I0135559

EMPIRE

The Coming Christian Conquest of the World

Third Edition

Russ Neal

Published by Innovo Publishing, LLC
www.innovopublishing.com
1-888-546-2111

Providing Full-Service Publishing Services for
Christian Authors, Artists & Organizations: Hardbacks, Paperbacks, eBooks,
Audiobooks, Music & Videos

EMPIRE: THE COMING CHRISTIAN CONQUEST OF THE WORLD

Available at http://empirethebook.com

All scripture is quoted from the King James Version of the Bible, unless otherwise noted.

Library of Congress Control Number: 2017948816
ISBN: 978-1-61314-376-6

Cover Design & Interior Layout: Innovo Publishing, LLC

Printed in the United States of America
U.S. Printing History
Third Edition: September 2017

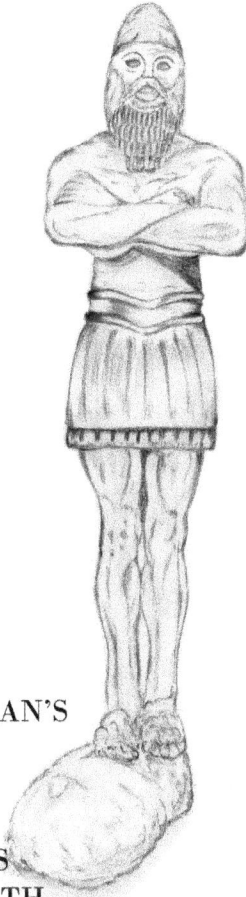

GOLD	BABYLON
SILVER	MEDO-PERSIA
BRASS	GREECE
IRON	ROME
IRON AND CLAY	DIVIDED KINGDOMS
STONE CUT OUT WITHOUT MAN'S HANDS	JUDGMENT
STONE FILLS WHOLE EARTH	CHRIST'S KINGDOM

Daniel's Succession of Empires

CONTENTS

Introduction 9

Part I: Knowing God **13**

The Inescapable Revelation of God in Nature 14

The law of God 15

The Uniqueness and Authority of the Bible 17

The Problem of Evil 18

Damnation and Salvation 19

The Witness of Jesus Christ 20

The Logical Necessity of the God of the Bible 22

Discussion Questions 24

Part II: A Christian View of History **25**

What About the Here and Now? 25

Philosophies of History Compared 25

The Stone Cut without Hands 27

The History of the World in Three Easy Lessons 30

Lesson 1: Creation to Christ *30*

Lesson 2: Church History *40*

Lesson 3: Modern History *50*

The Christian View of History, Summarized 60

Discussion Questions 62

Part III: The Nations Under His Feet..**63**

The Ruler of the Kings of the Earth.............................. 63

His Present Absolute and Universal Dominion 63

Church and State 64

What a Conquered World Will Look Like...................... 67

The Form of Government.. 68

Social Policy.. 71

Law and Justice 71

Economic Justice.. 73

International Relations 79

Free Speech 82

Biblical Law and Freedom 83

Discussion Questions 83

Part IV: Hot Topics **85**

Abortion 86

The Homosexual Political Agenda 87

Christian Persecution.. 89

Education 90

Part V: The Future and the End **93**

Our Present State 93

"But I Thought Jesus Was Coming to Take Us Away?" 94

Warfare Worship.. 96

Predictions.. 97

Conclusion.. 101

Discussion Questions 102

Appendix A: Salvation 103

Appendix B: The Baptism with the Holy Spirit 107

Appendix C: The Church 113

Appendix D: Classical Eschatologies 117

Appendix E: Economics 119

Appendix F: The Witchcraft of Words 123

Appendix G: Resources 129

Index 131

INTRODUCTION

SHOCK THERAPY FOR THE CHURCH

The Supreme Court's decision in *Obergefell* on June 26, 2015, supposedly discovering a hitherto unknown right to same-sex marriage hidden in the fourteenth amendment, created shock waves in the American Christian community. It needn't have. The committed course of the American people and especially its elites away from the law of God and gospel of Jesus Christ had been obvious to all, at least since the Court's similar discovery of a right to child killing "emanating from the penumbra" of the same document in 1973.

THE CHURCH LOSES INFLUENCE

Even more dismaying for the church than the external political defeats has been the internal bleeding of membership. With relatively little effective evangelism and a turning away from the faith by the millennial generation, the raw numbers of church-going Christians has been steadily declining. Neither fasting and prayer nor glitzy programs have had much effect in reversing this trend. Christianity, it seems, is just swimming against the tide of the times.

The enemies of the church have been particularly gleeful about this development, lovingly rehearsing statistics and anecdotes about the church's declining influence. Immigration policies designed to dilute the significance of conservative Christianity have been implemented, exacerbating the numerical trend. The overall Christian experience has become one of holding on as best we can while slowly losing.

COMMON RESPONSES

The response of church leadership in the face of these developments has been less than inspiring. The *escapist church* continues to cling to the end times view, interpreting the rise of evil as evidence of the end and holding out hope for imminent rapture. The *conformist church* is trying to make peace with the devil by downplaying moral concerns and trying to make the enemies of Christ buddies by being *nicer than Jesus.*

Even the most conservative and faithful are taking an entirely defensive posture by suggesting that we hunker down in quiet Christian enclaves to weather the storm, as if our enemies will allow such an option. Others try and push things like a First Amendment Defense Act (FADA) or Religious Freedom Restoration Acts (RFRA) as if the now triumphant people who hate us care about freedom of speech or freedom of religion, or as if the same courts that gave us child killing and the desecration of marriage will suddenly be sensitive to these niceties; as if tolerance was a two-way street.

DIAGNOSIS AND CURE

To properly diagnose what has been happening and identify the cure, we must start with bedrock biblical truth.

First, the only hope for our nation, any nation, and all mankind is the law of God and gospel of Jesus Christ, preached by the Holy Spirit–empowered church. Mankind is lost in slavery to sin on the inside. This will always result in slavery to other men on the outside. No political, military, or economic program to fix the outside problem can succeed until the inside problem is fixed. No humanistic philosophy or ideology is up to this task. The only fix for the inside problem is the gospel.

Second, the pass or fail test for the church is its testimony of Jesus, and more particularly, of *who Jesus is.* The church will succeed or fail based on the fidelity of her testimony concerning the person of her Lord. This testimony is our salt, our savor in a diseased world.

Third, God will judge any church that loses its savor, which fails to bear true and faithful witness to the person of Jesus Christ. Such a church is good for nothing but to be cast out and trodden under the feet of men.

From this it follows that the decline of our nation stems from the fault of the church, that this fault is related to our inadequate testimony of who Jesus is, and that God is handing us over to our enemies as a result.

In what way has our testimony of who Jesus is been inadequate? How is it we have failed in our primary mission? The answer is blindingly simple. We have failed to proclaim the *total lordship of Jesus Christ*. We have confessed instead a *limited* lordship, wherein Jesus is the Lord of the personal life of the believer, if you accept him, but is not Lord at all of those who choose not to accept him, and hence not Lord at all of human governments and the public life.

Here is a quote from one prominent pastor following the *Obergefell* ruling. His views are common if not dominant:

> *"[O]nce you get past [thinking America is a Christian nation]…. Once you begin to understand that democracy—that a republic actually—is designed to be an overarching system to protect our unique nuances, then we no longer look for public policy to reflect biblical ethics."*

The public life we hold is governed by man and his incarnation, the state. In matters of public life and law, "we have no king but Caesar." Worse, this government, like the old Roman Empire, is an overarching system with rule over the parochial beliefs of the little religious systems like Christianity under its umbrella. Such a republic is not under God; it is God. Someday in the future, maybe Jesus will come and be public as well as private ruler, but for now, Jesus has no right to intrude upon the affairs of men and nations who reject him. This is our confession. It is a polytheistic confession of two gods: Christ and Caesar. And when push comes to shove, we place Caesar above Christ. It is heretical. It is of no advantage to the kingdom of heaven for such a church to survive. Rather, such a church is an obstacle to the advancement of the gospel. This is why we receive no help from heaven.

The solution to our problem is, therefore, just as blindingly simple. We must recognize our error, repent of it, and adopt a true, full, and faithful confession of the total lordship of Jesus Christ. This will necessarily involve confronting our society about sin and rebellion. Of course we should then expect persecution and suffering, but these things are endurable if we know we are suffering for Christ and not for our own follies. We gain further consolation from knowing it all works to the advancement of the gospel in history and to our ability to hear him say, "Well done, good and faithful servant. Enter into the joy of your Lord." And we gain further encouragement yet when we know we are on the winning side in history. If we want to be part of the "Church Triumphant" on that great day, we have to be part of the "Church Militant" now.

IN THIS BOOK

This book argues for the view that the church is to evangelize and conquer the world for King Jesus, a view of victory in time and history. It is divided into a number of parts and appendices. The chapters have study questions at the end to facilitate group study.

Parts

1. Knowing God: Basic philosophical questions
2. A Christian View of History: Seeing the progress of God's plan in history
3. The Nations Under His Feet: What a conquered world will look like
4. Hot Topics: Abortion, homosexuality, persecution, education
5. The Future and the End: Predictions

Appendices

A. Salvation
B. The Baptism with the Holy Spirit
C. The Church
D. Classical Eschatologies
E. Economics
F. The Witchcraft of Words
G. Resources

PART I:

KNOWING GOD

You already do. Everyone does. It is not just in foxholes that there are no atheists. The knowledge of God is innate and universal, and there is nowhere in Creation you can turn your attention to and not be confronted with the Creator. Even if you close your eyes and stop your ears and are sensible of nothing but your own thoughts, you are still confronting God through His creation.

> *"Wither shall I go from thy spirit? Or whither shall I flee from thy presence?" (Psalm 139:7)*

The person who says "there is no God" is not just confused or mistaken; he is engaged in willful self-deception. He is in denial and lying to himself. There is something he knows full well even as he denies it. Surveys consistently show that only 4 percent of people say they are atheists. This means 96 percent of people believe in God and 4 percent are lying. Jesus said in John 3:17-18 that man's condemnation stems from the fact that, although light has come into the world, men loved darkness rather than light, because their deeds were evil. Man denies the light, not because it is not there, but because he prefers to continue his rebellion against God.

At the naval battle of Copenhagen in 1801, Lord Nelson's superior hoisted a flag signal ordering him to withdraw. Nelson reputedly placed his spyglass up to his blind eye, said he saw no such signal, and continued with his attack. In the same manner, even though God's revelation is open to man, man looks at it with a blind eye in order to be free to do as he pleases.

Rebellion against God is the common condition of mankind. All are in rebellion against God as a consequence of original sin. On the one hand, as God's creature made to walk with him and serve him, man desires God. On the other hand, as a sinner who wants to be his own god and his own ultimate authority, man avoids God. This is what lies at the root of all man-made religions. Man wants God, but on his own terms. Religious man seems to worship God, but his man-made religion only serves to keep him from the real thing. The real thing involves submission of the creature to the Creator, which rebellious man refuses to do.

THE INESCAPABLE REVELATION OF GOD IN NATURE

The Bible says that the invisible things of God are known to man by the visible things of Creation.[1] It does not say the doctrine of Creation is merely a better explanation of life's complexity than evolution. It says that Creation absolutely and incontestably reveals the Creator to man.

Consider the position the so-called modern atheists try and defend. They admit they have no explanation of how life might have formed without God. Spontaneous generation of life from non-living chemicals has never been observed in the laboratory or in nature, and no one can offer any plausible theory of how it could happen. Nonetheless, they very confidently claim that anyone who does not accept that life did and does form without God is an ignorant and dangerous religious fanatic and "science denier." They recognize that the whole universe seems fine-tuned to make human existence possible and openly worry that this might point to a creator. So to avoid this obvious conclusion they posit a near infinite number of other invisible universes, for which we have no evidence, all formed

---

1. Romans 1:20

by chance, and the one fine-tuned for life is of course the one we happen to be in. These people then say anyone who does not accept this story is unscientific.

The endless "Creation versus evolution" debates are ultimately foolish. Does it make any sense to have God as the supplicant before His creature, presenting evidences and arguments before man as the ultimate judge? Man strokes his chin, considering his decision, while God shuffles His feet nervously, awaiting the answer. Is this picture not insane?

There is also nothing new in the Darwinian tale of a self-creating creation. We think this was some sort of discovery in the mid-nineteenth century, but the idea of a self-creating cosmos, albeit in different terms, was common to the pagan world of antiquity. Ancient Greek ideas about creation had a role for a kind of god, a "demiurge," in creation, but also held that matter and "forms," or idealized patterns of things, were equally eternal. They later viewed the demiurge as more of a cosmic mind. The Romans saw chaos as giving birth to life which then evolved into higher forms. All of these amounted to a belief in a self-creating creation, the essence of evolution.

Today, there are so many different theories of evolution, including Neo-Darwinism, Lamarckism, punctuated equilibrium, life starting in the sea, life starting in the clay, life starting on rock crystals, life starting somewhere else and falling to earth in meteors, and space aliens with strange powers, that it may be truly said that evolution is just the theory that God did not create the world. The evidence is open to all, but not all are open to the evidence.

THE LAW OF GOD

When people argue about what ought to be done, they use the language of "right and wrong." In doing so, they implicitly acknowledge the existence of a moral law to which we are all bound. When God gave the written law to Moses, he said that one of the distinguishing features of the Israelites which would impress all other nations would be the quality of their laws.[2] This alludes to the fact that all men have an internal awareness of what the moral law should be and that this internal

---

2. Deuteronomy 4:8

awareness would enable them to recognize Israel's law as God given. The book of Romans says that "when gentiles do the things required by the law, they are a law unto themselves."[3] Even those without the God-given Mosaic law have an innate sense of it.

The moral consciousness resident in all men bears witness to a pre-existing law above all men, and hence to the ultimate lawgiver, God. Unbelievers will sometimes argue that they are more moral than many professing Christians. Far from being an argument against the existence of God, this confession of an internal moral sense on the part of professing unbelievers is itself proof of God's existence.

In spite of this universal knowledge, fallen man is at war with God. Desiring to be his own god and lawgiver, man resists and fights against any testimony to God's law. Sinners are never content to leave people alone who will not join them in their sin. Such people are a witness against them and their sinning, so they will pressure them to join in. For example, two doctors who refused to inseminate an unmarried lesbian were sued and recently lost in the California Supreme Court, 7-0. Cake bakers, photographers, and florists are forced to participate in the desecration of God's holy institution of marriage as a condition of participating in the economic system and feeding their families. Sinners cannot tolerate others not participating in their sin, because it stands as a testimony against them witnessed to by their own consciences.

Even in the church, many who fear the disapproval of man avoid preaching God's law, preferring to emphasize grace and forgiveness. But without the law and the threat of judgment, what is salvation? What is man saved from, low self-esteem? This negative attitude toward the law is called *antinomianism* and is in stark contrast with the attitude expressed by David in Psalm 119:97, where he says, "O how I love thy law, it is my meditation all the day." The law of God, rightly understood, is not a bunch of oppressive rules and regulations; it is the condition of man's life. The law of God is to man what water is to a fish. As God's creature, man is made to live in His law.

Many Christians hold a negative view of God's law. They argue that since we are "not under the (Mosaic) law" we are not under

---

3. Romans 2:14

God's law in any sense. With respect to the law, there are two equal and opposite errors. The first is *legalism*, or salvation through keeping the law. In the past this has been a common error in fundamentalist and evangelical churches, with emphasis on extra-biblical laws about dancing or drinking or clothing. The second is *antinomianism*, or a general negative attitude toward the law, a spirit of lawlessness in which reliance on grace and love makes all sorts of non-biblical behavior acceptable. This error, perhaps in reaction to excesses of legalism, seems to dominate the church today.

If we have the same attitude toward the law David demonstrated in Psalm 119:97, we will see the moral righteousness communicated in the law as a revelation of God's own character, a character to be emulated by his people. Those with this attitude toward the law will find themselves meeting and exceeding the requirements of the law without even trying.

Legalism is an attempt to force external observances on essentially rebellious and unredeemed people to *buy God off*. It is salvation through rule keeping. The issue here is not legalism. The issue is the righteousness required by God's law. The redeemed live on every word that proceeds from the mouth of God. All of God's word is law to man.

THE UNIQUENESS AND AUTHORITY OF THE BIBLE

The revelation of God in nature and moral consciousness is referred to as "general revelation." His revelation to Israel through His word, given by Moses and the prophets, and handed down today in the Bible, is referred to as "special revelation" and is much more detailed, clear, and explicit.

Although it is sometimes said that there are many bibles in the various religions of the world, this is not true. The Bible is unique in literature. Ancient writings of other civilizations are not comparable. The Bible consists of sixty-six books, written over two thousand years by some forty authors. Yet it reads as the one divine revelation it claims to be. It consists primarily of human history, recorded as a matter of simple fact, in contrast with other ancient pieces of literature that tell fantastic tales of demigods and monsters. It today stands alone as the serious alternative to the naturalistic narrative of the unbelievers.

Other books that claim similar authority would include the Koran and the Book of Mormon. These, however, are transparent imitation bibles. They originated long after the Bible had established its widespread recognition as the word of God. They are typically written by one man and are styled after the Bible. They are seldom defended against modern criticism since unbelievers do not take them as a serious threat in the first place.

As an example of the power of the Bible, consider the case of Massab Yousef, son of Hamas leader Sheikh Hassan Yousef, who converted to Christianity after reading the Bible. He found the command to "love your enemies" especially moving after being brought up to hate those he was told were his enemies. These words and others spoke to something deep in him, to the very innate knowledge of God. Now he gives bold testimony to his faith in Christ and prefers the name Joseph. His story is typical of millions.

There are many lines of argument defending the veracity of the Bible as God's Word. It has been defended against critics who cite other historical documents or archeological findings and against the so-called higher criticism that purports to find evidence in the internal text that certain authors did not write certain books. The arguments and findings which have been advanced in defense of the scriptures are mountainous and impressive, and mastering them is a worthy study. Proving that the Bible is the Word of God, however, ultimately becomes like the argument about God's existence. As God's Word, the Bible speaks to man with power and authority. It is self-authenticating, and, as John Calvin said in his *Institutes*, is not in need of "proofs or probabilities."

THE PROBLEM OF EVIL

Many who find the revelation of God in nature persuasive stumble on the problem of evil. This problem is usually phrased as, "How can a good God let bad things happen to good people?" The short answer to this question is, "He doesn't." There are no "good" people. All men are lost sinners, estranged from God by their inherited sin and their own particular sins, and destined for eternal destruction. It is only by the

Lord's mercy that this fate is held back during this period of grace so that some may be saved.

The contrary view, that all men are basically good, except maybe Hitler, merely reflects how lost mankind is. People see their "minor" sins as outweighed by their goodness. They see their unbelief, ingratitude toward God, lack of piety, disregard for the welfare or feelings of others, inordinate lusts, selfishness and sloth, as no big deal. Man is just so used to his sinful state that he thinks it normal. Such thinking mirrors that of murderers in prison who look down on the child molesters.

It is true that in relative terms what appears to be injustice in the suffering of good people and the prosperity of bad ones is commonly seen. But what is this observation if not envy and coveting, if not an impudent questioning of the wisdom of God in His dealings with us? Who is man to charge God with injustice? Does not the very fact that man does so add to his condemnation?

Even if the apparent lack of justice in the world were accepted as an argument against the existence of God, it would do nothing to answer the argument from design in nature or moral sense. Perhaps God exists and is unjust. (Just what standard against which the creator of all things could be judged, and where to find such a standard, is another problem.)

Accepting that God is just, that even unexplained suffering of relatively good people will all work out for good in the end, requires faith. Whatever is not of faith is sin. God is not obliged to answer every assault on His justice by His enemies. Man is obliged to put faith and confidence in him, come what may. It is not as if the Bible, with its accounts of the sufferings of Job, the prophets, and even Jesus himself, tries to candy coat it.

DAMNATION AND SALVATION

It remains true that in this life we see unpunished sin and unrewarded righteousness. The same internal sense of right and wrong that points us to the existence of God's moral law (and hence the existence of God) cries out for justice to be served, if not in the here and now, then in the hereafter. Every time we even think, "Darn that guy," which, to be honest, we do quite often, we are affirming our belief in some sort of final justice in the hereafter.

Think about it. What if that's not true? What if justice in not served in the end? Then all this talk about right and wrong is nonsense, and that leads us down the path to seeing everything about life as ultimately meaningless, including discussions about the meaning of life. It would seem that if even the possibility of meaning is to be preserved, we must assume divine justice beyond the grave.

Most religions approach the question of salvation and damnation *legalistically*, as a point system, where you hope your good points for good deeds will outweigh your bad points for bad deeds. We hope God grades on a curve and comfort ourselves that at least we are not as bad as some people. But does this make sense? What standard would a holy God use for judgment and for settling our eternal fate but perfection? Can any of us ever hope to meet that standard? Are not the universal sufferings and injustices of this life a warning that we are not OK in God's eyes, and that we are in fact under his wrath right now?

And yet in the midst of current suffering, there is also sunshine. There are deeds of mercy and blessings from heaven. After all, he hasn't sent us all to hell yet! What does all this point to? It tells us that even though we are damned, there is still hope; hope not from man or from our efforts but from God's intervention on our behalf. While there is life, there is hope. That hope is this: God sending His own Son as a sacrifice, paying the debt we could not pay, and making us right before God based on our faith in Christ Jesus, the Lamb of God that takes away the sin of the world.

THE WITNESS OF JESUS CHRIST

A recurring theme in human history is the need for a man-god, someone to bridge the gap between heaven and earth, between man and God. In his suffering, Job wishes for an intermediary, someone who could bridge the gap and adjudicate between man and God.

> *For he is not a man, as I am, that I should answer him, and we should come together in judgment. Neither is there any daysman betwixt us, that might lay his hand upon us both. (Job 9:32-33)*

This role has typically been seized by a king or an emperor, a purported man-god to rule both the religious and political sphere, both church and state. It has also been filled in myth by heroes and titans, offspring of human women and male "gods." The need for someone to fill this role is universal, seen in current politics with the elevation of one "Great Leader" or another to messianic level. If you visit Beijing, China, you will see the Forbidden City, home of China's ancient man-god emperors, the site where heaven was said to meet earth. Today it sports the image of Mao Tse-Tung, with his enormous mausoleum across the street in Tiananmen Square. It seems even atheists need a man-god.

The Christian faith is distinguished by the unique person of Jesus Christ, the true intermediator between God and man, the Son of God and Son of David, "the desire of all nations," 100 percent God and 100 percent man, joined in one person, yet with no mixture of the two natures. Perfect union without confusion, being the classical formulation.

While Jesus is indeed a great teacher, as other religions have great teachers, what distinguishes him is the centrality of who he is and what he did in history, rather than his teaching. Born of the Virgin Mary, suffered under Pontius Pilate, crucified dead and buried, risen from the dead and ascended into heaven, coming to judge the living and the dead; this, rather than his ethical teachings, is the confession of the church.

We thus have in Jesus the fulfilment of "the desire of all nations" in a manner totally satisfying of our need, yet totally unexpected by our philosophies. What other religious figure ever offered a solution for our sins and separation from God by offering his own human body as a propitiation for sin?

> *Having abolished in his flesh the enmity, even the law of commandments contained in ordinances; for to make in himself of twain one new man, so making peace; And that he might reconcile both unto God in one body by the cross, having slain the enmity thereby. (Ephesians 2:15-16)*

The fact of Christ's coming and His work in history makes any unbelief untenable.

The Logical Necessity of the God of the Bible

Basic to every system of thought is a group of axioms or *presuppositions*, which are held to be so basic that they themselves do not require proof. All reasoning proceeds from these starting point assumptions. They are held essentially as a matter of religious faith.

The humanist assumes that man and the universe he finds himself in are a lucky accident, a "fluctuation in the quantum field" that gave rise to energy and matter that luckily coalesced into galaxies, planets, and living beings. He may assume that our reasoning and senses "evolved" from some random processes, leaving the mind of man the highest authority in existence.

Alternatively, a Christian assumes that the universe and man were purposely created by a personal God who himself stands apart from his creation. He further assumes that as creatures we have no independent means of gaining knowledge. The biblical creator God must give his creature revelation as a starting point or basis for knowledge. The knowledge of God is the foundation for all other knowledge.

If one grants the Christian his presupposition concerning God, the Christian has a basis for knowledge. His senses tell him about a real world, and his reasoning faculties are valid because the creator God ensures it. All of his knowledge is necessarily contingent on the truth of his presupposition. His knowledge is valid, but dependent. This is called a *dependent epistemology*.[4]

The humanist by definition cannot tolerate a dependent epistemology. He must assume an *independent epistemology*, or he is not a humanist. He assumes therefore, an impersonal, self-creating or self-existent cosmos in which he is but a lucky accident. What then guarantees the validity of his senses or his reasoning? Why would an impersonal cosmos care? If all evolution cares about is survival, why would this necessarily lead to a creature with objectively valid reasoning? Of what survival value is abstract reasoning to a hairless ape? Assuming his presuppositions are correct, he is left with no valid way of knowing anything. His knowledge is independent, but also invalid.

---

4. Epistemology is the branch of philosophy that deals with the problem of knowledge, or "how we know what we know."

Another way of saying this is that atheism is self-refuting. If the universe was what the atheist says it is, the atheist himself, a thinking, feeling, choosing person, could not exist. The atheist demands proof of the existence of God when he himself is the proof. If the universe is ultimately impersonal, and we are just part of that universe, then we are ultimately impersonal as well, and our supposed thoughts, emotions, and will are all illusions, surface phenomena, no more real than the man a passing cloud might resemble.

It is therefore necessary to assume the existence of the biblical God for man to have a valid epistemology. This conclusion has far reaching implications. If all knowledge is based on revelation, then all of our private and public decision making ought to be biblically based. Man in his rebellion against God will find this conclusion unacceptable, but he has no logical reason for doing so and no valid alternative. His alternative is not only invalid given biblical assumptions; it is also invalid given his own assumptions.

How then do unbelievers engage in perfectly valid investigations and scientific discoveries if they do not have a valid theory of knowledge? The simple answer is *inconsistency*. They "borrow" the believer's assumptions without admitting it, even to themselves. Reason cannot be used to prove the validity of reasoning. Reasoning itself is an act of faith: of faith in the validity of reason.

The revelation of God is thus certain and absolute. Man is without excuse. Because of man's sin, however, this knowledge is only enough to condemn him. Salvation requires an additional work of God's grace.

This book highlights three key points or rules that are critical to understanding a Christian view of human government. The first rule identifies the dependence of human thought on divine revelation just discussed:

> *RULE 1: Man has no valid independent epistemology. Thinking itself is an act of faith.*

Again, one consequence of this rule is that all decisions about law and government must be based on God's revelation, which is to say, based on the Bible. There is no valid alternative.

DISCUSSION QUESTIONS

1. If the knowledge of God is innate, why do so many people deny it?

2. Why isn't belief in God the same thing as believing in the equally unseen "Flying Spaghetti Monster?"

3. How do we know that the apparent design and purpose in nature isn't just something we project on nature with our minds?

4. How is treating God as self-existent and eternal any better than treating nature as self-existent and eternal?

PART II:

A CHRISTIAN VIEW OF HISTORY

WHAT ABOUT THE HERE AND NOW?

Given our knowledge of God's existence, omnipotence, and purposefulness, what are we to make of human history? God must have a plan and a reason for making things or letting things go on as they have and as they continue to transpire. What are we to make of our own lives and how they fit into God's plan?

PHILOSOPHIES OF HISTORY COMPARED

History is philosophy. History is a record of what has happened, but historians are not just recording machines, indiscriminately writing down everything that happens. Some events are deemed more important than others. The events are filtered and organized in some way or in some pattern that reflects the writer's philosophy of history.

One common philosophy of history is the "great man" view. According to this view, history is contingent on the great man appearing at the right time. Without Julius Caesar, Roman history would have been vastly different. Without George Washington, there would be no

America as we know it. Another view is the "impersonal forces" theory. Changes in weather patterns, the invention of new technologies, and random events, are what drive history. Personalities may affect details, but the major thrust is controlled by these impersonal forces.

Since at least the time of Karl Marx, those on the political left have been obsessed with the notion of "historical inevitability." This views history as some sort of God-substitute, an impersonal force that is going to vindicate the leftists over time. "The arc of history is long but it tends toward justice," where justice is defined as the left's fantasies being fulfilled. "You want to make sure you are on the right side of history," meaning the winning side of history, meaning the side of the political left. The internal contradiction here is the notion that an impersonal force can have a right and a wrong side in the same sense as a personal God.

"Full of sound and fury, signifying nothing." So does Shakespeare, in Macbeth, invoke another popular philosophy of history, namely that it is a purely random affair without cause or meaning. Or as is often said, history is just "one darn thing after another." This is perhaps the most common view of the post-modern era. The devolution of humanistic philosophy into its present decrepit state, where our greatest thinkers strive only to prove the invalidity of great thinking, will be discussed in detail later in this book, but the view that history has no meaning is quite widespread.

Many evangelical Christians take a view of history not much better than this cynical one. They treat most of history as essentially meaningless and unworthy of study, except for the history in the Bible. Current events are studied only for signs of fulfillment of end times events believed to be predicted in the book of Revelation. Their view of the history of other nations and the period from the early Church until recent times borders on being deistic; as if God was uninvolved in these events.

For the Christian, the only proper view of history is the **providential view**, in which God is in absolute and detailed control. A sparrow does not fall to the ground without the Father's involvement, and even the hairs of our head are numbered.[5] Great Nebuchadnezzar, ruler of all Babylon, is forced to eat grass like an ox until he acknowledges that the

---

5. Luke 12:6-7

heavens rule.[6] God works all things, not just some things, according to the council of his own will and for his purposes. This means that we can study every aspect and every detail of human history and current events and see the hand of God at work, if we have the heart and mind to do so.

God's predestination of history is often thought to conflict with the idea of individual free will. This is an imaginary conflict. Man can and does have limited but real free will. God can and does legitimately hold man accountable for the exercise of this free will. The power, wisdom, and foresight of the One who spread out the heavens is so great, however, that man's free will is no obstacle to God's absolute control of history. The matter is similar to that of subtracting any finite real number from infinity. What is left is still infinity, but the finite number is still real.

THE STONE CUT WITHOUT HANDS

The key to understanding human history lies in Daniel 2:31-44, which tells of the "stone cut without hands" that (1) destroys the pagan idol, and (2) grows to be a great mountain that fills the whole earth.

In biblical terms, a nation is a group of people united by blood, language, and religion. An empire is a political structure that seeks to impose an umbrella government over many nations. The first attempted empire was that of Nimrod at Babylon after the flood. The plan was to build a tower to reach heaven, such that people would remain unified and not be scattered. It was an attempted preemptive empire, before mankind was divided into nations. To be sure, the people probably did not think their tower would actually reach heaven. It was likely an astrological observation tower. Nonetheless, man trying to build a tower to heaven is a perfect picture of the underlying spiritual reality. This reality was one of man trying to get back into his lost paradise through his own works and efforts. God intervened supernaturally by dividing the languages of united mankind and scattering them into separate nations across the face of the earth. His reason for doing this was to put a limit on the evil that could be done with a total consolidation of power. It was on the playing field of divided nations that God began to work out his plan of salvation by calling out a single nation, the Hebrews, as a people of his own (see Acts 17:26-27).

---

6. Daniel 4:26

Much later, during the Babylonian captivity of the Hebrews, Nebuchadnezzar had a dream of a great statue. The head was of gold, the chest and arms of silver, the belly of bronze, and the legs of iron. The feet were iron mixed with clay. This statue stood until a "stone cut without hands" fell from heaven and struck the statue in the feet, destroying it. The stone then went on to become a great mountain and fill the whole earth.

Daniel was given the interpretation of the dream. The simple summary is as follows: The statue represents four great empires that would rule over that part of the earth, central to the outworking of God's plan. The golden head was Nebuchadnezzar himself and the

Babylonian empire. The gold shows the purity or absolute nature of Nebuchadnezzar's god-like rule. The silver chest stands for the Medo-Persian Empire of Cyrus and Darius. Their kings exercised slightly less perfect power in that they were bound by the unchangeable nature of their law system. The bronze belly represents the Hellenic Empire of Alexander the Great, which mixed Greek ideas of democracy with Persian ideas of divine kings. The iron legs are Rome, strongest of the empires, yet with even more ideas that served to challenge absolutism.[7]

The steady degradation of quality from gold to iron conveys another meaning. The dream of a worldwide empire is idealistic. By subduing all of the warring, petty little nations under the majestic and enlightened rule of the empire, headed by its divine or semi-divine emperor, the empire would bring peace, justice, and prosperity to earth. The idea of global empire in that sense aspires to do something that meets a very real need, but it also involves an insane idea of a human divinity having absolute power over all other men. It proposes to eliminate the consequences of

_____

7. A government of absolute unlimited power

man's sin while keeping and even increasing the sin itself. The decline in quality from gold, to silver, to brass and iron, and finally iron mixed with clay (earth), shows the progressive collapse of the original ideal into a cynical position of raw power for its own sake. The split into two legs and then ten toes shows the increasing tendency of these systems to unravel.

The state of the world under Caesar Augustus was a spiritual nadir. Poets and philosophers despaired of life and mankind's future. Greek democracy and the Roman Republic had failed. Even the Jews who had the law, a God-given structure of government, and the prophets had lapsed into a dead Phariseeism. All hope for mankind seemed lost.

It was at this spiritual low point and the pinnacle of human imperial power that Jesus came. His intervention in history "in the fullness of time" was exclusively the work of God, making him the "stone cut without hands." His coming shattered not just the Roman Empire but the whole rotten idea of human empires.

In Mel Gibson's movie *The Passion of the Christ,* there is a scene in which Mary, the mother of Jesus, comes down an alley and sees her son Jesus beaten and disfigured almost beyond recognition, stumbling under the weight of the cross. Overcome by the injustice and brutality of it all, and moved by maternal compassion to reach out to her son, Mary approaches him. Looking up through the blood and the pain, Jesus looks at her and says, "Behold, I make all things new."

The passion of Jesus was history's ultimate game changer. All of the old rules of might and power were thrown out. True power was shown in submission to God, letting him work out his plan instead of man trying to impose his own. The fatal blow was struck at the real internal problem of man's sin and separation from God instead of just treating the external symptoms of injustice, division, war, and poverty.

And what does the scripture say concerning this stone? After utterly destroying the idea behind humanistic salvation-empires, it grows to become a great mountain filling the whole earth, the true salvation-empire. A mountain in the Bible symbolizes political power. This vision clearly says that the Christian Empire will bring all nations under its sway. What the humanistic empires had aspired to do, and failed, would be accomplished by God with his chosen King. Injustice, war, sickness, and poverty, would all recede as the stone grew into the greatest of mountains.

> *It shall come to pass in the last days, that the mountain of the Lord's house shall be established in the top of the mountains, and shall be exalted above the hills; and all nations shall flow unto it. (Isaiah 2:2)*

Nations will not be obliterated under the Christian Empire. Much of their national identity and diverse characteristics will be preserved, but all will be under the sway of the Christian faith. Not everyone will necessarily be Christian, but the law of God and the gospel of Jesus Christ will be the dominant influence on earth.

THE HISTORY OF THE WORLD IN THREE EASY LESSONS

This review of the history of the world from the providential perspective shows how God's plan of redeeming the earth through Christ and his called people has progressed thus far. It is offered as an example of how history can be so viewed.

Lesson 1: Creation to Christ

The Bible starts with a simple assertion of God's creation of the heavens and the earth by his word. The bottom line in the Creation-evolution debate is this: did God create the world and us, or did it all just happen? If he created it, then he is also lawgiver and judge. If it all just happened, and there is no creator, then there is no meaning, no ultimate right and wrong, no final judgment, and no need for a Savior. Man is free do what he wants precisely because nothing means anything. He can be responsible to himself alone, which is to say, completely irresponsible.

The term *evolution* may have many shades of meaning academically, but in the political sphere it is just the assertion that God did not create the world. Politically, evolution is nature worship as a substitute for worshiping God. It ascribes to nature all of the creative activity that Christians ascribe unto God. When a Christian worships, he goes into church and says to God, "You have created all things; it is from you we receive all blessings," etcetera. This is exactly the praise and honor that an evolutionist ascribes to nature.

The Creation account also gives us our first look at the triune nature of God.

1. The Father wills,

2. the Son agrees with the Father's will and says "let there be" light and stars and fish and everything else, and

3. the Spirit is released to move in power and make it so.

Thus there is an equality of essential divinity between the three persons (the Ontological Trinity) and a subordination and order in their working (the Economic Trinity). This is in contrast with Unitarian ideas of an "intelligent creator" or a "prime mover" common in non-biblical creation ideas. The peculiar Christian doctrine of the Trinity proves to be not a philosophical problem, but the solution to many philosophical problems. The triune Creator has interpersonal love and communication as an inherent quality. The Father, Son, and Holy Spirit communicate with each other and love each other. So great is the love between the three persons of the Trinity, that they are just as truly one as three. This is why we can say that God is love and that there is only one God. Creation is both an event and an ongoing project of God. The Father is active in original Creation and in its subsequent unfolding in history. His will is realized in history through the unique person of the Son and the diverse manifestations of the Spirit.

The Creation account tells us that man's original job description was "gardener."[8] A gardener takes mastery over the rest of Creation and makes it better than its untended state. He glorifies the owner of the garden by his faithful management. Man begins to take dominion over the rest of Creation by naming its creatures. Dominion is first an intellectual enterprise involving naming and making lists to achieve order and understanding. This model of man as a gardener contrasts with the currently popular "green" view of man as the enemy of nature, with nature in its untouched state being the ideal, with man's only duty being to minimize his footprint on mother earth, with low (or zero) human population as desirable. It also contrasts equally with any idea of irresponsible, selfish, or short-term misuse of the earth.

---

8. Genesis 2:15

The key points about Creation are summarized as follows:

1. God made us and the world. As Creator, he is also lawgiver and judge of his creatures.

2. God is uncreated, an eternal being. Everything else, including the universe, man, angels, and demons, is a created being. Between the Creator and the creation, there is a radical discontinuity. The creation is something separate from God, not just an extension of his being. This is the primary meaning of God's *holiness* and why God alone is worthy of worship by the creature.

3. Creation is both an event and a project. God is no "clock-winder" deity. He remains actively involved in the smallest details of creation and history.

4. The universe is personal. Man never deals with an impersonal cosmos but always with the personal Creator when we deal with his creation. Even the so-called "laws of nature" are not ultimately impersonal forces. They are merely a description of how God works most of the time. Exceptions are what man calls "miracles."

5. Evil is personal. Satan is a real person, a fallen angel, and an adversary with whom man must contend. Evil is not an abstract quality of man which we merely personify as the devil. Satan and his demonic host are real personal entities, working against God, yet under his ultimate control. Resisting sin involves a personal struggle against this enemy.

6. God is triune. Father, Son, and Holy Spirit all worked together and continue to work in Creation. God's qualities of one-ness and three-ness are equally ultimate.

7. The Creation is likewise triune, reflecting its creator. Space has three dimensions. Time is experienced as past, present, and future. Our understanding of particle physics holds that matter is made of three fundamental groups of quarks and leptons. Gravity, nuclear strong, and electroweak are the three known forces in nature. Efforts to reduce these three forces to some hypothetical single force have been unsuccessful or purely theoretical.

No other creature in all of creation is found to be a suitable helper for man, a help "meet" for him in his task of taking godly dominion over the earth. God creates a woman out of man and for man. The fact that she is originally taken out of man is the reason a man must leave his father and mother and cleave to his wife and be one flesh. The two again become one, and out of this union comes new human life to replenish the earth and subdue it. The triune God is thus imaged in mankind where the two are united in love such that they become one, the power of new life is released, and the work of dominion proceeds. It is because God has thus ordained the union of man and woman to represent the triune Godhead that marriage is holy. Adultery, fornication, incest, same-sex marriage, and every other unlawful sexual union desecrate that which is holy and are therefore major transgressions.

Note also that before the fall, the whole world was not yet subdued by man. In the Creation account in Genesis, God created Adam and Eve and placed them in a garden which he had planted in Eden. God blessed them and told them to be fruitful and multiply and to fill the earth and subdue it. He also gave them the responsibility to "cultivate and keep" the garden in Eden. So at this point—and before Adam and Eve had sinned, causing our sin nature and separation from God—the whole earth had not been subdued by man as God had directed. And as a consequence of Adam and Eve's sin, God's directive to be fruitful and multiply and to subdue the earth became more difficult. To Eve, God said,

> *Unto the woman he said, I will greatly multiply thy sorrow and thy conception; in sorrow thou shalt bring forth children; and thy desire shall be to thy husband, and he shall rule over thee. (Genesis 3:16)*

To Adam, God said,

> *Because thou hast hearkened unto the voice of thy wife, and hast eaten of the tree, of which I commanded thee, saying, Thou shalt not eat of it: cursed is the ground for thy sake; in sorrow shalt thou eat of it all the days of thy life; Thorns also and thistles shall it bring forth to thee; and thou shalt eat the herb of the field; In the sweat of thy face shalt thou eat bread, till thou return unto the ground; for out of it wast thou taken: for dust thou art, and unto dust shalt thou return. (Genesis 3:17-19)*

"Ye shall be as God, knowing good and evil."[9] Original sin enters when the devil tempts the woman and she is deceived with the promise of independence from God through an independent knowledge of good and evil. Adam, though undeceived, willfully joins in the sin. Mankind's original and continuing sin is thus the desire to have independent knowledge in order to be, for all practical purposes, his own god, which is to say, his own ultimate authority. In short, original sin is self-deification. This attempted ascension to divine status is, however, an insane dream that leads to death. Desiring to rise to the status of God, man falls below the status of "birds and beasts and creeping things" as he gives way to nature worship and sexual perversion, losing all of his power of dominion.[10]

However, even as man is ejected from the Garden, God gives hope. Man's sin leads to shame over his physical nakedness, which is symbolically associated with his guilt over sin. Man seeks to cover his nakedness with fig leaves, but God provides coverings of animal skins, signifying the inadequacy of man's works and the necessity of a substitutionary blood sacrifice. He promises the woman, through whom sin entered, that she will bear a seed that will crush Satan's head, even though Satan will bruise this redeemer's heel. Here the first glimpse of how history will unfold is revealed. God will move in the council of his own will and wisdom to bring forth the Savior. Satan will savagely oppose God's plan, but in the end he will be crushed.

The second man on earth, Cain, kills the third man, Abel. Why does he commit this crime? It is because he repeats his father's error in trying to please God. His vegetable sacrifice, like Adam's fig leaf, represents his own works. Abel's animal sacrifice, like the animal skins God provided for Adam and Eve, required the shedding of blood, recognizing the need for a vicarious sacrifice. Abel understood and accepted his inability to be justified by his own prideful work. Cain did not.

The period from Adam to Noah is the period of antediluvian[11] man with his famous nine hundred year lifespans. Some regard these life spans as symbolic, falling just short of a symbolic ideal lifespan of one thousand years. Others regard them as literal, reflecting a state of

9. Genesis 3:5
10. Romans 1:23-24
11. Antediluvian = before the flood.

man and nature not yet so burdened with accumulated sin. The scripture covering this time is brief, but the period is fascinating. Modern people no doubt have less difficulty with the idea of Jonah being swallowed by a whale than with real people living so long, but there is also a large body of extra-biblical information indicating the existence of ancient civilizations with fantastic achievements. People living for such a lengthy time would have been able to accomplish great feats, and if the history of mankind is more one of decline from a perfect created state than an ascent from animal-like existence, it might explain these early advanced civilizations. The pyramids of Egypt and Central America exhibit unbelievable engineering and yet date back before 2000 BC. Ancient sea maps showing correct longitudes of the Americas and Antarctica without its ice cap seem to have existed. It also appears that our whole system of the zodiac and its signs can be traced back to this time. Jewish tradition holds that it was developed by Adam's son Seth and was originally used to describe God's plan for the ages. Its present form represents a corruption by subsequent pagan civilizations.

For purposes of this book it is important to note that during this period, there was no civil government. Cain feared others would kill him for murdering his brother, but God placed a "mark" on him and prohibited anyone from doing so. Lamech killed a man for wounding him and invoked this prohibition on vengeance to keep anyone from killing him. The result of this lack of retribution was that earth was so filled with violence that God was moved to destroy it with a flood. Only Noah and his family were spared.

Immediately after the flood, God establishes a covenant with Noah, naming the rainbow as a sign of his promise to never again destroy the world with water. He repeats the covenant he made with Adam, with two related additions. Whereas antediluvian man was not authorized to use capital punishment against murderers (Genesis 4:15), Noah and those after him are commanded to do so. "If any man shed blood, by man shall his blood be shed" (Genesis 9:6). Man is also told to eat meat. This additional level of man's dominion over the dumb beasts symbolizes the rule of the righteous over the sinner. The Bible's dietary laws are better understood as symbolic of changes in the scope of man's dominion than as health rules.

After the flood, mankind is scattered into nations through the confusion of their languages at the tower of Babel. God then calls out one man, Abraham, and through him brings forth a chosen nation, Israel. Through Israel he brings special revelation, and ultimately the Savior, into the world.

The history of God's dealings with Israel makes up the bulk of the Bible. The focus of this book will be on the implications of these dealings for human government. Up until the exodus from Egypt, the government of Israel was that of an extended family. This family-oriented society found itself in a historic conflict with a child-killing nation ruled by Pharaoh, a man who claimed to be a god. He would not be the last man-god to be destroyed by the true and living God.

The Tower of Babel

Under Moses, the family nation receives the law of God at Sinai, beginning with the Ten Commandments. The Ten Commandments should be seen as not just as a summary of the law, but as a covenantal decree of God's special status as their king, and Israel's special status as his chosen people.

Judges and officers shall you have in all of your gates. (Deuteronomy 16:18)

The governmental structure established for Israel involved judges and officers (a judicial and executive branch) in each city, with a system of appeals up to a supreme judge who was also often the nation's military leader. Absent from this system was any legislature. The law was already God given. It was the role of the Levites to teach the law of God to the people. The people were not to just grudgingly obey this law, they were to study it, love it, teach it to their children, talk about it when they stood up and when they sat down. They were to totally internalize it and have their thinking completely changed by it. The judges and officers were to be men who feared God and hated unjust gain. As individuals who had internalized the law of God, the judges were to apply the law of God to cases. The officers were to carry out the decisions of the judges. The more difficult cases were to be appealed to higher judges, with the hardest being appealed to the national judge.

> *The Lord is our* judge, *the Lord is our* lawgiver, *the Lord is our* king; *he will save us. (Isaiah 33:22)*

The three natural branches of government were, at the human level, divided among the Levitical priesthood, the officers, and the judges. The only place where all three elements of government came together was in the Lord himself. Sovereignty was thus not located anywhere on earth but in heaven alone. It is the natural tendency of all human systems in rebellion against God to devolve into a system with a man-god as sovereign. God is everywhere and at all times at war with such systems. The destruction of these systems is one purpose of Christ's coming into the world.

This Mosaic system of government lasted (according to Paul in Acts 13:20) about 450 years through the book of Judges, ending with the last judge, Samuel. The people came to Samuel and said, "Give us a king like all the nations" (1 Samuel 8:5). They foolishly blamed their military defeats not on their apostasy, but on having God, rather than a man, as their king. God warned them through Samuel (and by supernatural signs) that their request was evil and that the king they demanded would oppress them, but the people refused to listen. God directed Samuel to anoint Saul as their first king. In spite of this major act of rebellion, God promised to bless them provided they and their king continued to follow his law. Saul was followed by David, "a man after God's own heart," and by David's son, Solomon. Both David and Solomon typified aspects of the coming Savior, who, humanly speaking, descended from their bloodline. A long sequence of kings followed, delivering mixed, but mostly bad results, until sustained apostasy led to the Babylonian captivity.

It was during the Babylonian captivity that Daniel received his revelation concerning the sequence of empires to come and the final coming of "the stone cut without hands," which is Christ. The Medo-Persian Empire conquered Babylon during this time. The Persian king Cyrus allowed the Jews to return to their native land after the seventy years of captivity predicted by the prophet Jeremiah.

The period from the return from captivity until the coming of Jesus saw the world empire of Persia replaced by the Hellenic Empire. (During this Greek rule, the revolt of the Macabees and the origin of Hanukah occurred.) There followed a descent into the dead legalism of the Pharisees and the ascent of the Roman Empire, the penultimate empire foreseen by Daniel.

It was at this nadir of history, with the Jewish world an old wineskin and the pagan world a cynical power state, a world in which it seemed impossible for the human soul to feel it had any worth, that Christ, the long awaited Messiah, the seed of the woman, the son of David, the stone cut without hands, came into the world. He came in the most unexpected manner imaginable: born of a virgin, laid in a manger. Eastern astrologers were somehow able to "see his star in the east" and discern his coming. When they inquired of the teachers of the law in Herod's court, they got the right answer: "in Bethlehem of Judea." But these very teachers of the law somehow missed the event themselves, so low was their spiritual state. Born in the most humble of circumstances, he was nonetheless King of kings and Lord of lords. His coming changed everything. It was the pivot point of history, the end of ages past, and dawn of the world to come.

The Jews, and even many of Jesus's own followers, thought their problem was the external oppression of the Romans. In this they typified all of mankind, which always blames its problems on others and never on their own sin. The Jews looked for a savior like the judges of old, a military leader to throw off the external oppressor. They did not understand the true nature of man's oppression. "He will save His people from their sins."[12] It is the internal oppression of man's slavery to sin, to rebellion against God, and to self-deification that leads to external

---

12. Matthew 1:21

forms of oppression. All previous judges and kings who had saved Israel from its enemies only foreshadowed this coming true salvation.

As was foretold from the time when Adam was given animal skins to cover his nakedness, and from the time of Abel's acceptable sacrifice, as was taught in the animal sacrifices of Mosaic law, without the shedding of blood there is no forgiveness of sin.[13] Christ, fully God and fully man, in the flesh, took upon his sinless self, upon his very human body, the sin of the whole world to become our true blood sacrifice. The veil of the temple, separating sinful man from holy God, was torn from top to bottom (symbolizing that the work originated from heaven), opening the way for man to come into God's presence. In teaching his disciples to pray, he told them to begin by addressing the omnipotent, eternal creator of the universe as "our Father." The fear of a remote and terrible deity was replaced with the security of knowing a loving Father.

The physical resurrection of Jesus Christ from the dead demonstrated the completeness of his victory over sin. The sting of sin is death. The last enemy to be overcome is death. It is through fear of death that man is held in bondage. No longer must man fear those who can kill the body, and after that have nothing more they can do. Where now is the power of the humanistic empire? Will they crucify the believer? Feed them to lions in the arena? Will the man-god Nero burn the disciples to illuminate his garden parties? So what? "If in this life only we have hope in Christ, we are of all men most miserable."[14] The believer's hope is in heaven, where his treasures are laid up, where no thief, no moth, no rust can touch them. A Christian looks for the sure hope of the resurrection of his own individual body; however, his enemies might torture, disfigure, and destroy it, even as they did to the body of the Lord. How is this statue of gold, silver, bronze, iron, and clay supposed to survive such a crushing blow to its ultimate power? How will the gates of hell resist the advance of a church, of a called out people, infused with such a blessed hope?

---

13. Hebrews 9:22
14. 1 Corinthians 15:19

Lesson 2: Church History

Jesus told his followers that it was to their advantage that he would leave them in order that the Holy Spirit might come. The Son acts as the singular and unique manifestation of God in Creation. The Spirit manifests in diversity and plurality, indwelling and filling all believers, giving a variety of gifts, and empowering a diversity of ministries. It was the plan of God and the ministry of Jesus to enable and empower the church, his bride, the help "meet" (suitable) for him, the "called out" body of believers, to be his instrument for recapturing the earth from the enemy.

Apart from the work of the Holy Spirit in the church, there is no hope for the human situation. Apart from this influence, individuals move toward anarchy, and governments move toward tyranny. War, poverty, suffering, and misery are the normal state of sinful man apart from the grace of God, which is ministered through the church, empowered by the Spirit.

When Jesus ascended into heaven, his disciples had just one question: "Are you at this time going to establish the kingdom for Israel?" Jesus told them that this was not for them to know. They were to go to Jerusalem and wait for the coming of the Holy Spirit. They were to be his witnesses in Jerusalem, Judea, and to uttermost parts of the earth. Their idea was to wait for Jesus to bring about the final resolution of all things. His idea was for them, empowered by the Holy Spirit, to advance his kingdom on earth. Heaven was going to receive Jesus until the restitution of all things and they, empowered by the Spirit, were to accomplish that restitution by making disciples of all nations.

The Baptism with the Holy Spirit, being filled with the Holy Spirit, speaking in tongues, and the role of signs and wonders are a matter of some controversy in the modern church, but there can be no controversy about their role in the church's beginning. On the day of Pentecost, while they were obediently waiting for the promise of the Father in the upper room, there came upon them tongues of fire, and they all began to speak in other languages, proclaiming the Word of God boldly and publicly with great effect. (Appendix B contains a further discussion on the Baptism with the Holy Spirit.)

It was not too long before persecution of the church broke out in Jerusalem. God used this persecution to scatter the disciples and cause the Word to be spread throughout the Roman Empire. Concerning the spread of Christianity as recorded in the book of Acts and the Epistles, the following points are noted:

1. The Word encountered fierce opposition from both the Jews and the pagans.

2. In spite of this fierce opposition, the Word also found wide receptivity and was even said to have "turned the world upside down."[15]

3. There was a total reliance on the Holy Spirit both for direction and empowerment. Signs and wonders performed by the Spirit were expected and taken as validation of particular ministries.

4. The problem of faction and false teaching grew to be the major problem facing the apostles as the first century came to an end.

5. Church government seems to have consisted of a body of elders at the local church in the city, with trans-local apostles and prophets sent out from the church in Jerusalem in the manner of circuit preachers.

In the subsequent centuries, the church continued to grow, experiencing some periods of relative peace, but many times of severe persecution. The writings of the early church fathers show their continuing problem with false teaching and with more subtle intermingling influences of pagan thought. The early church also seems to have had an expectation of Christ's imminent return. The idea of taking over the Roman Empire and having to run it does not seem to have occurred to them.

Nevertheless, that is what happened. Rome was dying on the inside. Everyone was cynical. Few believed in the old gods or even the old virtues. The Roman belief system, like all humanistic systems of thought, contained a profound contradiction. They believed that the ideal was for order to evolve out of chaos. This view led to the famous Roman emphasis on discipline and their impulse for empire building.

---

15. Acts 17:6

However, they also believed that life came from that chaos, and that order brought death. The games and the gladiators were an attempt to create some "organized chaos" in a hope of spiritual revival. This failed, and the Roman emperors became desperate to breathe life into their empire. Looking around themselves, the only people who seemed to have that kind of internal fire were the hated Christians.

Whether it was because of such considerations or an actual vision of a cross with the words, "By this sign you will conquer," the emperor Constantine ordered his troops to affix a cross to their standards and won the battle of the Milvian Bridge in 312 AD. Subsequently, he issued the edict of Milan in 313 AD creating toleration for Christianity. His mother, St. Helena, was a Christian.

The Christian history of the Roman Empire from Constantine to the Empire's fall is quite complex. There were good times for the Christians, times of renewed persecution, and attempted pagan revivals. It does seem that in the preceding centuries, the persecuted Christians had understandably not given much thought to what they would do if they took over the empire before Jesus came back. What stands out about this period is the clash of Christian and pagan ideas. A continuing trend to blend these systems of thought led to many heresies and a continuing intellectual and spiritual battle against erroneous doctrine.

During the first millennium after Christ, the church expanded in three main directions. The first was toward the west into the Roman Empire. The second was toward the east, going as far as India and China. The third was south into Africa. Both the Eastern and Southern churches adopted views of the nature of the union of God and man in Christ that differed from what the Western church accepted as orthodox. These schools of thought were called Nestorian, Jacobite, and Monophysite, and were declared heresies in the councils of Ephesus and Chalcedon in AD 431 and 451. In later centuries, these churches were to be nearly wiped out by the rise of Islam. Subsequent Christian history therefore mostly developed from the western Roman branch, which was to experience a major division itself.

The split of the Roman Empire into east and west, with Rome and Constantinople as the two capitals, resulted in the church similarly splitting into the Eastern Orthodox and the Western Roman Catholic strands in the Great Schism of 1054 AD. Many think of the Roman Empire as falling in 476 AD but overlook the fact that the Eastern Empire continued as Byzantium for another thousand years, only falling to the Moslems in 1453. The achievements of this Christian Eastern Empire are really quite noteworthy, especially when the rest of the world had descended into a comparatively barbarous state. In many ways the Eastern church can claim a more linear and unchanged succession from the New Testament church. The question is whether that is a good thing. The Eastern church differed from the Western in the following key points:

1. They did not accept the primacy of the Bishop of Rome. Their bishops were viewed as equals, and their churches took on slightly different characteristics in the nations they dominated.

2. They placed more emphasis on a contemplative experience of God (theosis) than on academic doctrine.

3. They put great emphasis on maintaining early church traditions and tended to be backward looking.

4. They used icons instead of statues.

5. They did not accept the addition to the Nicene Creed of the statement that the Holy Spirit proceeds "from the Father and the Son" (the Filioque). They held that the Holy Spirit proceeds from the Father only. This view tends to diminish the essence of the Son relative to the Father.

6. In the Creeds they use the phrase, "We believe," while the Western church says, "I believe." This subtle change created a more argumentative and creative atmosphere in the west. The more interesting intellectual history was therefore to unfold in the west.

The most important western thinker of this time was St. Augustine. His writings were to establish the norms of Western Christianity for the next eight hundred years, the period later to be called the middle ages or the dark ages. These monikers are quite misleading. They are labels put on this period by Renaissance thinkers seeking to discredit the old ideas and advance their own.

Compared to the many errors common to his day, the thinking of Augustine was quite biblically sound. He strongly affirmed the authority of scripture. However, his thinking was also influenced by the popular Platonic philosophies of his time. This mixture of thought systems was to influence the next eight centuries and still has major influence today.

One example of how Augustine's thought was influenced by Platonism can be seen in his view of the six days of Creation. A modern man might assume that the founder of the dark ages would take a literal "six, twenty-four-hour days" interpretation of the Creation account, but this was not so. Augustine said that of course this six day language was figurative, just to make it easier for our mortal minds to grasp. Actually, he said, God being perfect and beyond space and time, an act of God such as Creation must have been instantaneous, taking not six days, but zero seconds! This view shows the influence of the prevailing Platonic thought of the world Augustine inhabited. (Without saying whether the world is actually 4.5 billion years old, six million years old, or six thousand years old, the Christian ought to pause to ask himself to what extent his thinking is influenced by the non-Christian thought of the world around him today.)

The influence of Platonic thought on Christian thinking is toward dualism. That is, the tendency to put things in one of two categories, spiritual or natural. The middle ages were influenced by this, with their division of much of life into "spiritual" and "temporal" categories. The same influence can be seen in much of today's Christian thinking. When one hears that "Christians shouldn't be involved in politics," or suggestions that full time Christian work is more holy than secular work, one is experiencing the continuing pagan influence of Platonism.

The much maligned middle ages actually did show considerable progress due to the influence of Christian thought, such as it was. The idea of Christ as the only ultimate king in heaven made the idea of the king as a man-god untenable. Kings and officials had to think of themselves and represent themselves as Christ's servants. The church and state each competed as separate power centers, with the tension giving the common man some breathing room of freedom. This was an early form of what is now called, "checks and balances." Kings were feudal lords, which in principle made their relationship to their people one of contract, that is, protection and justice in exchange for revenue and loyalty. All of this was a big improvement over the consolidated man-god of the pre-Christian and non-Christian world, to say nothing of the modern fascist or communist divinized state.

The middle ages also involved much more scientific progress than is generally recognized, especially in their latter half. Crop rotation and the invention of the wheeled plow greatly improved agriculture, for example.

The close of the middle ages and beginning of what we call the Renaissance can be marked by another famous Christian thinker, who sits like a book end to Augustine. Thomas Aquinas emerged as the early Renaissance was rediscovering many of the Greek and Roman works that had been neglected or suppressed. As Augustine was influenced by Plato, Aquinas was influenced by Aristotle. Where Plato emphasized the importance of universal truth and deductive reasoning, Aristotle emphasized the particular facts and inductive reasoning. Both, however, incorporate the unbiblical idea that man has a valid independent epistemology, which violates Rule 1.[16]

A sincere Christian, Aquinas sought to show that the truth of Christianity could be derived or proven

Aristotle teaching Alexander the Great

by reasoning without resort to biblical authority. His intention was to strengthen the Christian position, but his means of doing so placed human reason on a par with scriptural revelation. This opened the door to the whole modern world of humanistic philosophies.

---

16. Rule 1: Man has no valid independent epistemology. Thinking itself is an act of faith.

Humanistic Philosophy

Humanistic philosophy may be defined as the attempt to understand and explain knowledge apart from the revelation of God. As such, it has its origin at the fall of man, when the serpent's temptation was to "be as God, knowing good and evil." Most humanistic thought has maintained religious trappings, relying on invented gods, idols, myths, legends, and supposed religious teachings as sources of authority. The Greeks were just as religious as other cultures for the most part, but their civilization was the first to also give rise to purely humanistic philosophy as well. What makes the Greek philosophers unique in their time was their attempt to create a system of knowledge without reliance on any real or pretended revelation. Socrates, Plato, Aristotle, and the others developed systematic schools of thought, rather than the proverbs and sayings of other "wise men" of the pre-Christian era. Their philosophies were adopted and somewhat advanced by the Romans, until overtaken by Christianity.

From this time we can trace an intellectual battle that continues to modern times and defines Western civilization. It is a battle between Jerusalem and Athens; between the theistic and humanistic worldviews; between reasoning based on revelation and reasoning said to be independent of revelation.

From the point of view of the humanists, ancient man's mind was trapped in religious superstition until the Greeks made their breakthrough. The subsequent Christianization of the Greco-Roman world, marked by Augustine, was the beginning of the "Dark Ages," which lasted until the Renaissance, or rediscovery of pagan thought, marked by Aquinas.

From the Christian point of view, reasoning apart from revelation is an invalid project doomed to failure. It is essentially rebellion against God and an implicit assertion of divinity by man. The non-biblical religions of antiquity were man-made idols, pretend gods created by man to cover up the essentially rebellious nature of what they were doing. Only the chosen people had the true revelation of God in the law and the prophets. The Greek philosophical enterprise differed from the pagan religions only by making their implicit self-deification explicit. The philosophy of Augustine was consciously submissive to biblical revelation but did not make a clean break with the Greek philosophers.

The effort by Aquinas gave independent humanistic thinking equal footing with revelation and re-launched Western man's effort to establish an independent epistemology.

The next phase in this battle manifested in the humanistic Renaissance and the biblical Reformation. The Reformation took the view that Roman Catholicism had created a synthesis of Christian and pagan thought and sought to redefine a purely biblical system. Their success in this was significant—but incomplete. Western civilization as a whole is a synthesis of Athens and Jerusalem, and the Christian struggle to extricate its thought from pagan influence is one that continues to our present day.

Beginning with the Renaissance, the world of humanistic philosophy proceeded to develop through the work of a whole series of men. Each tried to knock down the arguments of their predecessors and put forth their own epistemological system. The earlier philosophers tended to pursue deductive approaches. That is, they took Plato's approach and tried to identify certain self-evident truths such as, "I think, therefore I am," and show how the whole body of knowledge could be logically deduced from these truths. It proved difficult to come up with any truths that were really self-evident. As a result, later philosophers favored Aristotle's more inductive approaches, arguing from a collection of facts and observations "uphill" toward universal truth. Inductive approaches are inherently problematic since all it takes is one new fact that does not fit the beautiful truth for it all to come crashing down. The Renaissance was followed by the Enlightenment, which became openly atheistic. In the French Revolution, which is closely associated with the Enlightenment, they even set up a prostitute as the "goddess of reason" at Notre Dame Cathedral, just in case anyone had missed the point.

In between and overlapping the Renaissance and the Enlightenment came our other major intellectual event, the Protestant Reformation. Dates for when each of these movements was dominant put the Renaissance from 1250 to 1500, the Reformation from 1500 to 1750, and the Enlightenment from 1750 to present. Although the Renaissance is generally seen as a revival of humanistic thinking in opposition to the authority of revelation, it also helped create the intellectual environment for the Reformation. The Reformation was a "back to the Bible" movement which sought to ground itself on the self-authenticating authority of the Bible. If the Renaissance was criticizing the Roman Church for being too stuck on the Bible, the Reformation was criticizing it for not being stuck enough. Support for the Reformation came from various kings, notably in northern Europe and England. They both believed this teaching and seized on it as a means of breaking from the power of Rome and the Holy Roman Empire. All of this did not happen without bloodshed.[17]

The Reformation thinking and worldview had a tremendous impact on Western civilization and can be credited in large measure with creating the intellectual environment which gave rise to all of the following, which today characterize Western civilization:

1. *The modern scientific revolution.* All of the following pioneers of science were either Protestants themselves or came from Protestant lands: Bacon, Newton, Kepler, Maxwell, Herschel, Joule, Kelvin, and Babbage.[18]

2. *Capitalism.* Calvinism in particular taught that one's trade was a "calling" as sacred as any church vocation. It also emphasized frugality. Hard work and saving naturally leads to private capital accumulation, which leads to capitalism. A frequently referenced book on the connection between Protestantism and modern capitalism is The Protestant Ethic and the Spirit of Capitalism by Max Weber.

3. *Excellence in the arts.* Composers such as Bach, Handel, Mozart, Beethoven, and the painting of the Dutch Masters exemplify this influence. Reformation thinkers saw all music, secular and sacred, as a gift from God. Truth and beauty were the focus of the arts, in contrast to today's emphasis on mindless sex, violence, and negation of meaning.

---

17. It should be noted that Martin Luther and his peers originally sought dialog and reform of the Catholic Church. They did not seek separation in the beginning. Ironically, part of the Roman Catholic Church's response to the Reformation was the Counter Reformation, which belatedly made many of the reforms and corrected the worst excesses which had provoked the Reformation in the first place.

18. See www.creationsafaris.com/wgcs.htm for a more complete discussion.

4. *The Constitutional Federal Republic as a form of government which balances order and freedom.* This revolution in seeing government as servant rather than master arose directly from the Protestant movement, as will be shown.

Guilt

Guilt is a pervasive aspect of the human experience. Human attempts to deal with the burden of guilty feelings lead to all kinds of unproductive and even counter-productive behavior. Some people try and deal with guilt by transferring it to others and assuming a victim role. They then "beat up" on the others endlessly. Others assume guilt for all sorts of things for which they are not guilty, or only marginally so, and "beat up" on themselves, hoping the excess punishment will somehow relieve their feelings of guilt. None of this is successful and only results in wasted effort and misery. This perversity can be seen in individuals, families, and nations.

People feel guilt because they are guilty. All men are guilty of sin before God, which no amount of transference or self-flagellation can change. Only the Christian gospel offers the true solution to human guilt. Jesus Christ took humanity's sin on himself on the cross. Through faith in his vicarious death and resurrection, man finds the only possible release from his guilt. Proceeding from this place of rest, release, and freedom, redeemed man goes on to productive work. No longer struggling to earn a forever elusive justification, he is free to realize his potential.

It is therefore unsurprising that so much of man's progress in science, economics, art, and government took place in those societies most influenced by the law of God and the gospel of Jesus Christ. This observation leads to the second rule for understanding the Christian view of human government:

> RULE 2: *Our internal salvation from sin, death, and damnation has external implications for every aspect of our personal and public life.*

This review of church history concludes with events in England, because it is in the story of the church in England and in colonial America that the idea of the Constitutional Federal Republic emerges. The way the Reformation played out in England was as bloody and convulsed as on the continent, but the struggle resulted in new thinking regarding the theory of civil government. Ideas in the sphere of church government had parallel developments in the sphere of civil government. Episcopalianism, for example, means rule by bishops (i.e., bishops appointed by the king). Presbyterianism means rule by elders (i.e., elected representatives). Congregationalism means, obviously, democratic rule by the local congregation. Struggles concerning the issue of church government are closely and logically tied to struggles in the area of civil government. The result in England was limitation on the power of the king and the development of a Parliament, which included a hereditary House of Lords balanced by an elected House of Commons, thus advancing the concept of governmental checks and balances.

Two important religious groups in England at this point were the Puritans and the Pilgrims. The Puritans were Calvinist reformers whose goal was to "purify" the Church of England. The Separatists, later to be known to us as the Pilgrims, saw no need to reform the Church of England. Why could they not just separate and form their own reformed congregations? The Puritans opposed the Separatists as "schismatics" who were dividing the body of Christ.

Lesson 3: Modern History

While this religious struggle was going on in Europe, an entirely new world was being discovered in the west. Christopher Columbus started a European exploration of the Americas with his famous discovery of 1492. Spain and Portugal, two Catholic countries with both a lust for gold and a desire to evangelize, led the way in this exploration through the planting of missions and staking of claims. England did not enter the competition until the Jamestown plantation of May 14, 1607, in Virginia.

The Pilgrims, the Separatists from England, came to America to find the freedom to worship as they saw fit. They were financed by private investors and accompanied by other English adventurers who were not part of their church. They had a governmental charter from the king for the plantation they were to establish near Jamestown. Navigation being what it was in those days, they ended up in Massachusetts. The non-church members indicated that, this not being the place designated in the charter, they were under no obligation to submit to any government in the new colony. Wanting to avoid the catastrophe such anarchy would bring, the Pilgrims authored the famous Mayflower Compact as a constitution for the colony's government. This providential event became a precedent in the American mind for the ability of a free Christian people to constitute a civil government without any royal sanction.

The Mayflower Compact

A short while later, the Puritans were themselves the victims of persecution in England and ended up migrating to Massachusetts. Once there, with no Church of England to purify, they adopted many of the self-governing attitudes of the Pilgrims. The later Catholic settlement in Maryland was to also take on some of this self-governing character. The Pilgrim colony was not particularly prosperous, and some of them moved on to establish Connecticut. Here they established a government using the Mayflower Compact idea of writing their own constitution, which they called the Fundamental Orders of Connecticut. This document incorporated many of the ideas that were later to be used in the US Constitution, which is why Connecticut calls itself "The Constitution State."

These governmental developments in England and America were extensions of the Reformation stream of thinking. Meanwhile, on the European continent, things were taking a very different turn. In France, Catherine de Medici[19] had the leaders of their Protestant movement, the Huguenots, liquidated at the St. Bartholomew's Day Massacre in 1572. Many of the survivors were later to flee and settle in the American colonies. Paul Revere and Alexander Hamilton were two of their descendants. The Huguenots, in addition to being Protestant, tended to be the middle class. Their removal left a void between the Catholic monarchs and the peasants, which the secular revolutionaries exploited. These secularists were children of the Enlightenment, a more radical extension of the humanistic thinking of the Renaissance, as previously discussed. Its influence was to dominate French and European thought up to present times.

The French Revolution is identified with the slogan, *"Liberte, Egalite, and Fraternite,"* or, "Liberty, Equality, and Brotherhood." The idea behind liberty included things like human rights and elective governments and had many similarities to classical liberal thinking in England. The idea behind equality was more of a universal leveling of classes and was the seed behind what was to become international communism. Fraternity or brotherhood was the idea behind Napoleon's "le Grand Nation" and was later to find expression in fascism.

Modern history is the outworking and interplay of two very different revolutions: the American and the French. The French Revolution and its offspring represent the humanistic strain of thought from the Renaissance and Enlightenment. The American Revolution represents a mixture of Reformation and some Enlightenment ideas. Today's American politics also roughly falls into these two groupings, with conservatism following Reformation ideas and liberalism going with the Enlightenment. Again we see Jerusalem and Athens.

In the period leading up to the American Revolution, from 1730 to 1770, there occurred in the American colonies a spiritual "Great Awakening." Preachers such as George Whitefield, Jonathan Edwards, and many others led large revival meetings in churches and open air venues. One effect of this movement was to cement Protestant

---

19. De facto ruler of France about from 1559 to near her death in 1589.

Christian thinking in the minds of most Americans by the time of the Revolution.

The American Revolution differed fundamentally from the later French Revolution and its European offspring. In many ways, the Americans thought of theirs as a conservative counter-revolution. The American colonists had established their own elected governments and operated them for 150 years with little interference from the home country. As England sought new revenue, she began to crack down on the colonies, taxing them "without representation" in Parliament. This the Americans saw as a revolutionary change depriving them of their established rights as Englishmen.

The American Declaration of Independence drew upon an interesting doctrine from the Reformation. This is the doctrine of "interposition" or "the lesser magistrates." The question often faced by the Reformers, and now by the colonists, was when and how a Christian might resist a law or command from "the powers that be." Calvin's answer had been that the individual can flee but never forcibly resist even an unjust act from the government. To do otherwise would be to invite a spirit of lawlessness and anarchy. This would go against Paul's teaching in Romans 13 and David's example in refusing to kill Saul, "the Lord's anointed," when Saul was unjustly trying to kill him. David instead continued fleeing from Saul until God dealt with the mad king. On the other hand, according to Calvin, duly constituted intermediate governments, the "lesser magistrates," have not only a right but a duty to "interpose" themselves between an unjust ruler acting contrary to the law of God, and the victimized people. This thinking also reflected the Christian doctrine of "Lex Rex" (the law is the King), popularized by influential Scottish theologian and writer Samuel Rutherford in 1644. Rutherford wrote to refute the contrary notion of "Rex Lex," which asserted that the king was the law. The word of the king is not law, Rutherford insisted. Rather the king is under the law and obligated to obey and enforce it, and by engaging in taxation without representation it was the king who was the true rebel.

These ideas, which seem elementary today, were revolutionary at the time. They were, however, a well thought out and faithful application of the doctrines of scripture to the situation. What we see happening is doctrines and understandings implicit in the law of God and gospel of Jesus Christ being worked out in history. It was an extension of the kingdom of God into a new area of application in accordance with our Rule 2.[20]

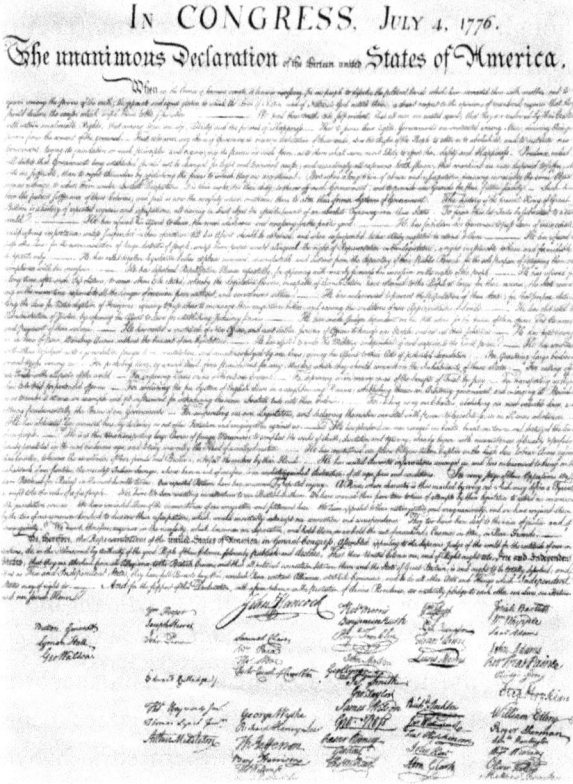

The Declaration of Independence

The US Constitution is rightly revered as one of the most important milestones in the history of human government. Recall one of the most important principles of government we have seen in biblical and church history: *sovereignty belongs to God alone.* Sinful man, being a slave by nature, gravitates to a man-god, a "king like all the nations," as his natural form of government. Redeemed man places his ultimate hope in God alone. He therefore sees government in a limited, ministerial role.

---

20. Rule 2: Our internal salvation from sin, death, and damnation has external implications for every aspect of our personal and public life.

Monarchies place ultimate power in the king, parliamentary systems place it in the Parliament, but the US Constitution places it in no individual or institution on earth. It is a system of checks and balances designed to resist the earthly consolidation of power. In particular: (1) Power is divided between the states and the federal government. (2) The federal government is given limited and defined powers under Article I, Section 8. (3) All other undefined powers are reserved to the states or the people. (4) The federal power is divided between the legislative, executive, and judicial branches. (5) The legislative branch has a House and Senate with features to balance each other. In this way the US Constitution is the first constitution since Moses to reserve sovereignty for God alone.

The Continental Congress at Prayer

The third and final rule for understanding the Christian view of human government can now be seen:

> RULE 3: A Christian form of government is "under God." It reserves ultimate soverignty to God alone. It resists the sinful tendency of man to consolidate power. If a government is not under God, it is god.

Modern Times

The modern humanistic philosophy project that began with the Renaissance and Enlightenment continued in the nineteenth and early twentieth centuries under the name of Modernism. Modernism was another attempt to achieve the goal of a complete and valid system of knowledge based on reason alone. Here again is the quest for an independent epistemology. World War I shattered much of the optimism about the ultimate triumph of man's reason. The modernist project was dealt an additional, some would say fatal, blow, with Kurt Gödel's "Incompleteness Theorems" in the 1930s. Gödel demonstrated that any axiomatic[21] mathematical system of thought would contain true statements that could not be proven from the axioms of that system. For example, it appears that every even counting number greater than two can be written as the sum of two prime numbers, but no one can prove this. Such proof requires resort to some more fundamental system, ad infinitum. Although this only applied to mathematics, it seemed to doom the goal of Modernism. If we cannot construct a complete and valid mathematical system, how can unaided human reason achieve certainty in other, more slippery realms of knowledge?

Kurt Gödel

The Christian should not be surprised or disappointed by this result. To the Christian, man's knowledge, while valid and useful for practical things and to be used to the glory of God, is forever dependent on revelation from the only Being with perfect and complete knowledge. Perfect God-like knowledge is forever beyond man's grasp. There is no "theory of everything" and never will be.

---

21. A system based on deductions from a set of unproven rules or axioms assumed to be true. Euclidian geometry is a common example.

The reaction of the humanists to the collapse of Modernism was not to humble themselves and return to God. Rather, it was to deny the reality of objective knowledge and objective truth altogether. This led to our present situation and what is called Postmodernism or Deconstructionism. In this system of thought, reality does not exist; rather, it is constructed in our minds and projected onto the world. The search for objective truth is abandoned, replaced by the "will to power." This is what lies behind all of the black studies, Chicano studies, women's studies, gay studies, and diversity education in our schools. In a world with no God and no objective truth, only the political power of the group matters. The group uses this political power to define and create the world as it wishes it to be. In this world there is no objective right and wrong, no place for the individual identity, and no sense in the individual seeking truth for its own sake. You are part of your identity group and nothing else.

This history of humanistic thought demonstrates the original thesis stated in Rule 1; that man apart from God has no independent epistemology. Upon discovering this, and given the choice between repenting and returning to God, or leaping into the abyss, man leaps.

The governmental history of the United States after the adoption of the Constitution for the most part runs contrary to Rule 3 in that it is a history of the consolidation of all power into the hands of the federal government and all of the federal power into the executive. It is a slow return to the system we had when King George tried to rule as an absolute monarch. A summary of these negative events follows:

1. The Civil War, fought to "save the union," did so, but only in a radically different form which shifted the balance of power from the states to the federal government.

2. The fourteenth amendment to the US Constitution transferred the basis of citizenship from the states to the nation. Whereas formerly, one was first a citizen of their state and by reason of that a citizen of the United States, now "All persons born or naturalized in the United States, and subject to the jurisdiction thereof, are citizens of the United States, and of the State wherein they reside." It also contains the vague "equal protection" and "due process" clauses, clauses that would later be used to create

all sorts of new "constitutional rights," rights which were actually transfers of power from the free individual and his state to the ever growing leviathan of the federal government. Even while it was being debated, the amendment was understood by many to be a massive transfer of power from the states to the federal government and was opposed even by some northern states. In order to pass it, Congress had to refuse to accept rescission of approval by Ohio and New Jersey and use its army to force occupied Alabama and Georgia to approve it.

3. In 1913 the sixteenth amendment was passed, authorizing the federal income tax. This diminished the states and strengthened the central government by giving the federal government the "first bite" on the income of individual Americans. It also gave the federal government a pretext for total knowledge of the private financial transactions of all individuals and the ability to control their actions with a myriad of tax incentives.

4. Also in 1913, under the seventeenth amendment, the election of senators was changed from a vote of the state legislature to a popular vote, again shifting power from the states to the federal government by muscling out the states as intermediaries between the people and the federal government.

5. The rise of the regulatory and administrative state moved more and more actual government from the constitutional branches directly accountable to the people to a secondary government only indirectly accountable. The regulatory state is a product of a political philosophy known as *Progressivism* which held that modern life was too complex for ordinary people and that rule by experts was better. Progressivism is in turn the product of Modernism.

6. The Commerce Clause, giving the federal government jurisdiction over "interstate commerce," has been stretched by Congress and the courts to give the federal government jurisdiction over almost everything, including a farmer growing food for his own consumption.

7. The radical idea that the Constitution has no meaning other than what the courts say it means emerged, making these courts virtually tyrannical. This is the doctrine of the *Living Constitution*, an imaginary document existing only in the collective mind of the federal judiciary and a cult of progressivist lawyers.

8. Courts rewrote the first amendment's non-establishment clause to impose a Soviet style separation of church and state doctrine. This doctrine goes far beyond separating the two institutions of church and state, relegating God and religion entirely to the private sphere and freeing government from the law of God. This divinizes government. If the American government is not "*under* God," then it *is* God. There is in principle no longer any limit to what the government can do to the people.

This progressive drift from a Constitutional Federal Republic with its checks and balances toward the consolidation of all power in a tyrannical central government may seem complicated and confusing in the details, but it is simple in its effect. When a Christian people fall away from their faith and their pastors and teachers fail to instruct them, fallen nature takes its course and chains result.

Alexis de Tocqueville, viewing the nascent American experiment in self-government, famously observed that the failure of such experiments come when the masses of people realize they can use their control over government to vote themselves money. Today in America, more and more people view the role of government as giving them their "fair share" of other people's money. If doing this means they must allow ever greater consolidation of power until they are completely enslaved, so be it. This is the fate of sinners in this world. Their fate in the next is even worse.

Increasing numbers of people today are adopting this sinful and slavish attitude of dependency because fewer and fewer pastors and church leaders are preaching a fearless gospel of repentance toward God and faith in Jesus Christ. Even those who do so preach limit Christ's lordship to the individual and affirm the civil government's independence from Jesus. The rise of liberty in America was due to fearless preaching, and its decline is due to fearful preaching.

Taking the Long View

At any point in time, things always look bad for Jesus. No one is listening to him. Church leaders and institutions look weak, compromised, and even corrupt. Everyone is cynical about politics. Economies are in trouble, war rages, injustice and inhumanity abound. It is little wonder that Christians despair and assume the end of the world is at hand. They think that all that is left is for Jesus to rend the skies and come down like *deus ex machina*[22] to fix everything. We are like nervous people at a bus stop in a bad neighborhood hoping the bus will come soon.

And yet, when we step back and take the long view, what do we see? Compared to the world the early Christians faced, the world today enjoys greater freedom and prosperity, sees man's dominion over nature advancing through science and technology, and even sees Christianity as the largest and fastest growing religion in the world. The whole thing looks so chaotic, and yet it is as if Jesus was actually in control, slowly spreading his kingdom across the earth.

The church is always losing in the short term and yet always winning in the long term. Consider the apostles. Paul described their experience as being like the captives at the end of a Roman triumph parade. He referred to the apostles as the "scum of the earth," and yet it was the kingdom the apostles were advancing that won out, not the one the Roman legions were defending.

The "stone cut without hands" has indeed dealt a fatal blow to human pretentions of empires and new world orders but is itself growing to be a "mountain that fills the whole earth," the true world Empire.

THE CHRISTIAN VIEW OF HISTORY, SUMMARIZED

In the beginning, God made everything "very good." Then sin entered, and with it suffering, sorrow, and death. Was God's "Plan A" frustrated, and was he forced into some kind of rescue "Plan B"? No. It was always God's plan to be glorified in the church, in the people he would redeem from such a horrible fate. The bride of Christ is not a

---

22. When ancient Greek playwrights wrote themselves into an irresolvable plot, they would sometimes have a god come down and fix things. The god was played by an actor lowered by a crane, the "god in the machine" or *deus ex machina*.

perfect "Stepford Wife."[23] She is a fallen, lost woman redeemed from death by her Savior and Lord, and not only saved, but perfected, for she shares in her Lord's sufferings and labors. She begins as the helpless victim rescued but goes on to be "a help meet for him." The task of pushing back "the gates of hell," of extending the kingdom of God on earth, is given to her. No longer prostrate and helpless, she stands on earth as the representative of King Jesus. Her prayers and worship rise to heaven and shape history. Like her Lord, she suffers persecution, but also like her Lord she rules and reigns. Those who persecute her suffer the wrath of God, both in this world and especially in the next.

This extension of the kingdom, of the Christian Empire, is wide, and it is deep. It is wide in that it applies to "all nations." Christians preach the gospel and seek the conversion of the elect out of every subdivision of humanity on every square foot of this planet. It is deep in that it teaches them to obey "all things" he has commanded. That is, every area of human activity, be it government, family life, medicine, business, education, art, or science, indeed "every thought," is being brought into obedience to Christ.

Salvation has three temporal aspects. When an individual comes to Jesus initially, he is completely saved once and for all. But he also "works out his salvation" as he lives and grows in Christ, a progressive work over time often called sanctification. And no matter how sanctified the believer becomes in this life, his salvation is not complete until the resurrection on the last day.

In the same way, Christ's redemption of the world system has three aspects. His First Coming, death, and resurrection saved the world. The progress of his empire through the Holy Spirit empowered church manifests the implications of his gospel in history. The final and complete salvation of the world occurs at his Second Coming in full power and glory. Having worked and suffered with him in history, his glorious bride takes her place at his side at the marriage supper of the Lamb, ruling and reigning with him for all eternity. History is the love story of Christ and his church. All other actors are merely playing supporting roles.

---

23. From a 1970s novel and movie in which men were provided with "perfect" wives who were actually robots.

History is to have a culmination. The church will conquer and emerge triumphant. The Empire will be extended over the whole earth and then the end will come. In the eternal state, the redeemed will not be angels flying around on clouds playing harps. They will have glorified bodies like Christ's resurrection body. They will inhabit a new earth under a new heaven, not subject to our present laws of decay and death.[24] As the bride of Christ, the redeemed will take their place at his side, sharing in his eternal rule.

History is not just one darn thing after another. It is the story of the church and her triumph in Christ.

DISCUSSION QUESTIONS

1. Does belief in biblical Creation require belief in a literal six days of creation and a global flood?

2. How does God's creating man male and female relate to the theme of Christ and his church?

3. In the first century, the gospel went into "all the world." Why did it seem to most prosper in Europe?

4. What aspects of the American republic are logical extensions of the gospel? Which aren't?

---

24. See the book *Heaven* by Randy Alcorn for a full discussion.

PART III:

THE NATIONS UNDER HIS FEET

THE RULER OF THE KINGS OF THE EARTH

Recapitulating, the three rules for understanding the Christian view of human government are as follows:

HIS PRESENT ABSOLUTE AND UNIVERSAL DOMINION

> RULE 1: *Man has no valid independent epistemology. Thinking itself is an act of faith.*
>
> RULE 2: *Our internal salvation from sin, death, and damnation has external implications for every aspect of our personal and public life.*
>
> RULE 3: *A Christian form of government is "under God." It reserves ultimate sovrignty to God alone. It resists the sinful tendency of man to consolidate power. If a government is not under God, it is god.*

Jesus is not only the ruler of heaven destined to also be ruler of the earth some day in the future. Revelation 1:8 plainly calls him the "ruler of the kings of the earth." He himself declared that all authority on heaven and on earth was given unto him. No earthly ruler can lift his hand or utter a word without his sovereign permission.

Psalm 149:8 says the saints are to bind the kings of the earth with chains and their nobles with fetters of iron. Psalm 2:3 has these same kings saying, "Let us break their bands asunder, and cast away their cords from us." It is the law of God that binds the kings of the earth. It is from his law they seek to free themselves to "be as gods." It is of this law that the church bears witness, binding them to its obedience.

CHURCH AND STATE

And Jesus answering said unto them, Render to Caesar the things that are Caesar's, and to God the things that are God's. (Mark 12:17)

Probably no verse in the whole Bible has been more misunderstood than this one. (See also Matthew 22:21 and Luke 20:25.) This saying of Jesus is commonly used to support the proposition that there are two separate spheres of government, each with a legitimate claim on our obedience. God has some sort of limited claim on our spiritual life, while the civil government has an independent claim on everything else.

Nothing could be farther from the truth. The prior verses 13 through 16 show that Jesus knew he was answering a trick question. The tax paid to Caesar was a tribute, a tax that acknowledged his claim to total sovereignty. If Jesus said to pay the tax, he would be agreeing with Caesar's claim and undercutting his whole ministry. If he said not to pay the tax, they could have him arrested. So he asked them whose image was on the coin used to pay the tax. Of course, it was Caesar's image. His indirect answer was to give what is Caesar's to Caesar and to God what is God's. The obvious point is that while the coin bore Caesar's image, Caesar and every other man bore God's image. Thus, without giving them an answer they could use to have him arrested, he affirmed that everyone and everything is subject to God, denying Caesar's claim to sovereignty.

God is the ultimate authority to whom everything and everyone is accountable. The notion that civil government or any other aspect of Creation has any degree of independence from his authority is an error of the highest order. God established three principle human institutions: the family, civil government, and the church. Each has its sphere of delegated authority and each has a symbol of that authority. The family is charged with training up their children in the way they should go. It is the principle economic unit and responsible for the care of its members. Its symbol of authority is the rod of correction.

The civil government is charged with executing murderers, with punishing those who do wrong and praising those who do well. Its symbol is the sword. Force is always an available option in life. At any time, anyone can get up and go hit someone else. God's institution of civil government means than man is charged with limiting the use of force to upholding righteousness through duly constituted and lawful institutions. This use of force is limited to enforcing a subset of God's law as defined in scripture. For example, hating your brother and hitting him are both violations of God's law, but civil government is only authorized to use force to remedy the latter.

The church is charged with making disciples of all nations. It is to proclaim the law of God and the gospel of Jesus Christ. It speaks prophetically to all areas of life. Through its teaching and preaching and administration of the sacraments, it leads men to salvation. Through its prayer and worship, it participates with God in the ultimate government of the earth. What the church looses in heaven is loosed on earth. What it binds in heaven is bound on earth. Its symbol of authority is the keys of the kingdom. Its visible use of these keys is through welcoming or expelling (excommunicating) members. By its teaching it equips the individual Christian to carry out godly dominion in his particular calling, and that calling may include civil government.

Each institution has its prerogatives and limitations. The family may not execute its errant members. The government may not use the sword to compel man's conscience, nor to advance evil in any way. Though the church speaks to all issues of life, it has no direct power beyond speaking the word, administering sacraments, and determining its membership.

Non-Christian societies tend toward the consolidation of all three institutions in one. Any of the institutions may be guilty of this, because the problem is in man, not in institutional structures. King Henry VIII made himself head of the Church of England. Several popes asserted their right to appoint and remove kings. The heads of cultic families seek to cut their members off from any influence of church or state. God established each institution and established its limits. We need to be mindful of those limits and fear transgressing them. Church leaders need to be wary of intruding too far into family matters. The government needs accountability to all of its citizens, not just to a large and powerful church. Heads of families need to understand the limits of their power. The civil government must recognize and honor the legitimate spheres of family and church. It is of course this last boundary that is most threatened today as the civil government seeks to grow without limit.

The Three God-Ordained Human Institutions	
Institution	*Symbol*
Family	Rod
Church	Keys
State	Sword

It is very plain what our courts and secularists mean when they talk about "separation of church and state." These words are found in the old Soviet constitution, not in the US Constitution. They are also taken out of context from a metaphor used in a letter by Thomas Jefferson to a group of Baptists to calm their fears that a unbelieving president like Jefferson might interfere with their religious freedom by telling them the first amendment prevented such government interference. The US Supreme Court took these words to mean that the church could not interfere with the state, which now declares itself to be independent of God in heaven. By separation of church and state, they mean, "get your church out of our state!"

However, Psalm 2 informs us that when rulers make such a declaration,

He that sitteth in the heavens shall laugh; the Lord shall have them in derision. (Psalm 2:4)

The assertions of divinity by mere men on the courts are indeed worthy of derision. God is the one seated in the heavens, but spiritually speaking so is the church. Therefore her attitude toward self-divinizing earthly authorities should be similarly dismissive. Psalm 2 goes on:

> *Then shall he speak to them in his wrath, and vex them in his sore displeasure...Thou shalt dash them in pieces like a potter's vessel. (Psalm 2:5-9)*

God starts by laughing at these rulers but He does not stop there. He goes on to judge their rebellion decisively. The mad intentions of these people will come to nothing as judgment falls from heaven.

WHAT A CONQUERED WORLD WILL LOOK LIKE

Theory is fine, but what would it look like in practice to bring civil government under the law of God and gospel of Jesus Christ? Do we have to start stoning people and stop eating lobsters? No. What we do have to do is start taking God's Word seriously and asking ourselves how it applies to us in our present situation. Modern nations are not in the same place as ancient Israel with its special calling. In fact the apostles specifically declared that the gentile Christians would not be told to keep the law of Moses except for prohibitions on eating meat with the blood still in it (i.e., living animals) and sexual immorality. Careful thought is therefore needed.

What is the fundamental relationship between religion, morality, and law? When people say, "you can't legislate morality," do they mean law is unrelated to morality? Are religion, morality, and law three unrelated topics as shown below?

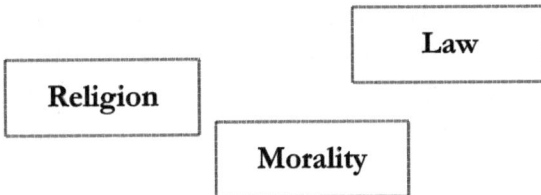

Law

Religion

Morality

Or is the relationship better shown by this diagram?

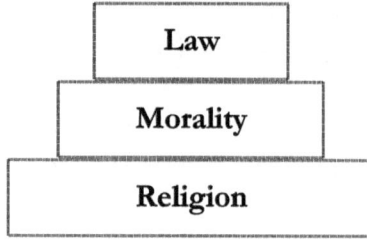

```
        Law
      Morality
      Religion
```

Law is seen to be based on morality, but morality covers more than just what is legal. When we say, "you can't legislate morality," we mean there is part of morality that lies outside the scope of law. Similarly, religion (or philosophy, or worldview) covers more territory than just moral teaching. It also speaks to such things as the nature of reality and the basis of knowledge.

Our task then is to do the hard work of thinking through what the teachings of scripture have to say about morality and law. This is called "theology." Theology involves three steps:

1. Studying the Bible as a whole to see what it teaches.

2. Thinking about how this teaching applies to any given subject like law or government.

3. Applying this thought process in practice.

The following sections are one attempt to do just that. Call it a theology of civil government.

THE FORM OF GOVERNMENT

What would be the form or structure of a government shaped in accordance with biblical law? Classically, three forms of government have been identified: (1) monarchy, or rule of one man; (2) oligarchy, or rule of an elite few; and (3) democracy, or rule of all. Any of these forms can be tyrannical.[25] We usually think of a tyranny in terms of monarchy or dictatorship, but oligarchies and democracies can be just as

---

25. Tyrannical means lawless government. A government subject to arbitrary human will rather than law.

tyrannical as monarchies. We have seen the Supreme Court try and act like an oligarchy, substituting their will for the written constitution, and we have seen lynch mobs in the street carry signs saying, "This is what democracy looks like!"

Rule 3 tells us that first and foremost, the form would reserve sovereignty for God in heaven alone; it would not locate sovereignty in any human being or human institution. It will therefore be characterized by divisions of power and systems of checks and balances so as to recognize God's ultimate sovereignty.

This was the idea behind the US Constitution and why it represents such an important milestone in the progressive Christian conquest of the world. It establishes a system of human government without locating sovereignty in any man, any group of men, or even in the people as a whole. Instead it creates a system of the rule of law, laws made by an inclusive process full of checks and balances, laws that apply to everyone, a government of law and not of men.

It achieves this end by means of dividing power first between the federal and state governments, and then by dividing the government into the three branches of executive, legislative, and judicial. It also staggers election times and lengths of office and includes many other barriers to the consolidation of power into any one set of hands—not that people have not tried and are not trying today to overcome these barriers and consolidate power, with varying degrees of success. This however, only shows the wisdom of the founders, operating within the biblical worldview of their time, in erecting such barriers. We must remember that a paper constitution, like any other document, can only do so much. If the people lose their Christian character, they will become "slaves on the inside" and will not only allow the barriers to be breeched but will demand their breeching until they become "slaves on the outside" too.

One important way in which we are losing this limitation on government is by our careless use of the term *democracy* or *democratic* to describe our government. Far from being a democracy, the form of government established by our constitution is a constitutional federal republic. This distinction matters.

The idea behind a pure democracy was summarized in the ancient phrase, *Vox Populi, Vox Dei,* "the voice of the people is the voice of

God." Thus, democracy as an idea is inherently anti-God and hence unchristian: the worship of the false pagan deity, Demos. Strictly speaking, democracy is when the people directly vote on the laws, as happens with initiatives. Making all laws by this process becomes impractical, so the people usually elect representatives to a legislature which in turn makes the laws. This is referred to as a republic. In general, parliamentary republics are strongly democratic. The most "democratic" of these have only a popular house which is subject to frequent elections. The parliaments choose the executive branch members (referred to as "forming the government") and can create and alter the judiciary at will. Such systems tend to be very volatile and frequently ineffective and are therefore prone to being replaced by dictatorships or military juntas.

The joke about democracy is, "one man, one vote, one time!" Less democratic forms add stabilizing features, such as England's now defunct House of Lords, a written constitution that is hard to change, and in some cases a vestigial monarch with some limited but psychologically important stabilizing influence. The US Constitution adds an upper house known as the Senate. Originally, senators were appointed by the state legislatures and only every six years (one third every two years). This constituted a stabilizing element to the more volatile House of Representatives. The volatile House is itself a check on the Senate becoming an oligarchy. In addition, the president is elected directly every four years and the Supreme Court members are appointed for life.

From a biblical point of view, the most problematic branch of government is the legislature. The problem lies with the question of the source and origin of law. Recall that the system of government established by Mosaic law lacked a legislature because the operative law was the law of God, given to Moses, and faithfully taught by the Levites. This teaching responsibility today belongs to the church. A human legislature can be taken to imply that man, rather than God, is the source and origin of law. In fact, this is why humanists like to talk about democracy rather than a republic. To humanists, democracy is the elevation of the pagan deity Demos, "the voice of the people," or, "the general will" of collective mankind in opposition to the true God of heaven, to serve as an engine of rebellion. They view the legislature as the incarnation of this abstract deity "Man." The Christian view of the legislature is that of a Representative Republic. In this view, the legislature is a representative committee system for making earthly laws in conformity with God's law, to balance the power of the executive and judicial branches of government, and to establish a government of laws rather than a government of men.

SOCIAL POLICY

The basic unit of social and economic order is the natural and extended family. Societies with intact natural families experience social order, peace, safety, and prosperity. Societies without stable families experience disorder, crime, and poverty. Sane governments seek to support the natural family. Modern secular governments, being suicidal, seek to undermine it.

Beyond the practical, the family with its husband-wife, parent-child, and other relationships are symbolically important to God's revelation. Violations of these relationships and their boundaries not only bring on the well-known practical consequences but also insult God, profane his holy ordinance, and invite his wrath. Biblical law focuses on maintaining and strengthening the family. Our public policy ought to therefore focus on strengthening the family unit and limiting activities which undermine it. Adultery, fornication, incest, abortion, and homosexual acts are all to be forbidden. Pornography would be outlawed as subversive literature. Divorce would be permitted but not encouraged as we do with our so-called "no fault" divorce laws, which are designed to favor the party at fault, encourage family breakup, and visit misery upon children.

LAW AND JUSTICE

The biblical system of law and justice is one focused on restitution, backed up by corporal and capital punishment. Imprisonment as punishment is unknown, as is rehabilitation in the modern sense. Forcing violators to make restitution to their victims provides all of the needed rehabilitative effect.

The purpose of punishment is to vindicate the moral law of God in the minds of the people. It is not meant to "reform" people or "deter" certain conduct, as if people were animals to be trained. People are moral agents made in the image of God. They are directly and individually subject to his law. When due punishment is given for violations of God's law, the offender feels he deserves the punishment and the victim feels vindicated. This reinforces God's law in their minds as well as in the minds of all the people. It is God's law in the mind of the people that provides true social order, not fear of punishment as such. When the legal system itself deviates from God's law, its efforts to enforce its decrees do not find support in the God-given consciences of the people. Such a society will require massive police establishments and cradle to grave brainwashing to maintain order.

For example, there was a time petty theft got so bad in England that pickpockets were hanged. Other pickpockets worked the crowds at hangings. Since hanging is not a deserved punishment for petty theft, the excessive punishment only made people more cynical with respect to the law. "Poor Benny, he got caught; too bad for him." The "rehabilitative" approach of the modern therapeutic state commits the equal and opposite error. The criminal is given rehabilitative therapy to find out why he feels he must commit crime. He plays along, seeing it as a game. His victims do not see the criminal getting the deserved punishment and feel like fools for obeying the law. In a biblically sound system those guilty of transgressing are given their "just deserts." Both the transgressor and society see this as justice and the law of God is vindicated in the public mind.

> *Because sentence against an evil work is not executed speedily, therefore the heart of the sons of men is fully set in them to do evil. (Ecclesiastes 8:11)*

Some particular features of biblical law and justice are worthy of note. Just how these principles would be applied in a modern society is a matter for debate, but the principle behind the provision should be honored.

1. Capital punishment could not be imposed without the testimony of two or more witnesses. Capital punishment for murder is mandatory, not optional.

2. The witnesses had to cast the first stone in execution, followed by all the people. A false witness could not escape being an actual "hands on" murderer.

3. Unsolved murders had to be ceremonially atoned for by local authorities who had to swear they knew nothing of the crime. Innocent blood was said to pollute the land, which could only be cleansed by the blood of the murderer. This ceremonial requirement reminded local authorities of their responsibility.

4. Murderers were also sometimes killed not by the authorities but by a relative of the victim, an "avenger of the blood."

5. In the case of an accidental death, the killer had to flee to a designated city of refuge to escape the avenger of the blood until the death of the high priest. That could be the next day or many years. The punishment, like the accident, was unpredictable and in God's hands.

6. Failure to obey the verdict of a judge was punished by death. Contempt of court was a capital offense.

7. Restitution was the goal of the legal system. A thief was required to restore four times the value of the thing stolen.

ECONOMIC JUSTICE

It is common today to criticize an economic system based on the difference in income and wealth between the rich and the poor. This rule is not only unbiblical but anti-biblical. The Bible tells us that righteous behavior and faithfulness is blessed, while sin and disobedience is cursed. Furthermore, the multi-generational accumulation of wealth by the godly was seen as a normal objective and consequence of obedience to God. A focus on disparities leads to coveting, which leads to institutionalized theft in the form of income and wealth transfer programs. These policies amount to taking money from people who earn it and giving it to those who did not earn it in exchange for their votes.

> *Do not show favoritism to a poor man in his lawsuit…Do not deny justice to your poor people in their lawsuits. (Exodus 23:2-6 NIV)*

The correct way to judge an economic system is not to measure disparities in wealth between the top and bottom ten percent but to ask whether it rewards good economic behavior or not. A system that rewards hard work, savings, and lawful behavior, and which punishes sloth, profligacy, and criminal behavior, is a good system. In this regard, radical disparities of wealth and income may be an indicator of underlying injustice such as "crony capitalism," where the connected prosper not from good economic behavior but from political connections and government favors. The solution is to end the illegitimate favoritism, not to maintain it and try to fix the consequences with income transfer. Two wrongs do not make a right.

He who gives to the poor lends to the Lord, and the Lord will repay him. (Proverbs 19:17)

Concern for the poor and a willingness to materially aid them is an important aspect of righteous living. The law commands that the poor and weak not be oppressed by the rich and strong. It does not authorize civil government to force the rich to give to the poor. This is a matter of conscience, faith, and faithfulness. Considering the account of the rich man and Lazarus in Luke 16, it is a matter of the utmost seriousness with God. No doubt, many a rich man who neglected the poor is burning in hell right now and more will be tomorrow. Although government is not permitted to punish the rich for failing to show compassion to the poor, God is well able to do so. In fact, a society in which the rich routinely neglect the poor is ripe for judgment, a judgment which may well take the form of a communist revolution.

Several aspects of our present economic system may be properly criticized as unjust, which is to say contrary to God's law and in need of reformation. Each fails the test of rewarding good economic behavior.

1. Our **monetary system** is not tied to gold or silver or anything tangible, or even to a fixed rule. This is done so that the money supply can be manipulated, ostensibly for the common good of regulating steady economic growth. It leads, however, to a situation in which the financial elite manipulate the money supply for their private gain. The people most hurt are the poor who are deprived of the ability to improve their situation by hard work and saving. Between taxes and inflation, saving yields a negative return. This is a conscious government policy that

should be reformed by a return to something similar to a gold standard. Taxes on some first amount of interest, dividends, and capital gains should also be eliminated to encourage thrift and industry.

2. Biblical law takes a very dim view of charging **interest**, especially to the poor. The law included a system of release from personal debt every seven years and of a return of encumbered family real property every fifty years. A fifty year mortgage is almost the same as an interest only perpetual loan. The idea seems to have been to prevent man from following his natural drift into debt slavery. In contrast, modern laws seem to be designed to encourage unlimited and permanent indebtedness. Debt, rather than gold, is the ultimate backing for our money. Return on corporate equity is double taxed, whereas return on debt (interest) is a deductible expense. Imprudent loans to poor people and poor nations are pushed, and when they are unable to repay the loan, schemes are hatched to have the taxpayer bailout both lender and borrower. Since budgets are never balanced, the taxpayer actually borrows the money to bail out both.

Most scriptural injunctions against charging interest on debt seem to have in mind lending to the poor. Borrowing money for your necessary food shelter and clothing is something no one would do in biblical times if it were not necessary to live. Charging such people interest was viewed as taking advantage of someone's misery for financial gain and was prohibited. Whether this same rule should apply to consumers seeking to borrow for luxury items is another matter, but the biblical system seems intent on minimizing societal indebtedness in general.

In the business context, the prohibition may not apply as strongly. In the parable of the talents, Jesus has the master condemn the slothful servant for burying his money in the ground instead of putting it in a bank for interest. Whether this story constitutes an endorsement of business lending in general is debatable, but lending money to capitalize a business is clearly different from lending to the poor so they can eat their next meal. It was clearly lawful to rent a house or some land to someone for a period of time. Why should it be unlawful to rent them the use of a similar worth of gold for a period of time? All business requires capital, and investors can either provide that capital in the form of equity or debt. Debt provides what is known as "financial leverage" and increases the potential profit and potential loss at the same time. Business owners decide how much debt financing to use based largely on their assessment of the risk they face. Riskier business will require more equity and less debt. When government policies encourage debt financing, as is the case today, businesses take on more debt than they otherwise would. This increases the volatility of our overall business cycle, causing much suffering of those who live from paycheck to paycheck.

3. The **welfare state** institutionalizes theft and creates dependency, often intergenerational dependency. Intended to help the poor, it has a near perfect record of harming them. The welfare state should be dismantled, but dismantled from the top down, beginning with welfare for the rich (crony capitalism), then welfare for the middle class, such as education and health benefits, and lastly welfare for the poor, replacing it with private charity.

4. One provision for the poor was **gleaning**. Land owners were forbidden to go over their harvest a second time to get any remnants. These were to be left for the poor who followed the harvesters, gathering enough to live by hand. Gleaning was hard work. Actually, any Israelite could take some grain or fruit from a neighbor's field to satisfy immediate hunger. They could not go through such a field with tools to harvest more than that. A modern application of this principle might be hiring poor people to do incidental work one could just as easily have done one's self. Modern employment and liability laws stand in the way of this practice by imposing excessive risk and cost on such casual employers.

5. A **monopoly** over any good or service allows the seller to command above market rates for what they sell. There is such a thing as a "natural monopoly," most commonly seen in utilities. Such monopolies are either made government functions or regulated. It is almost impossible for private parties to establish an unregulated monopoly without the help of the government. Unregulated monopolies are established by governments using various rules. Usually these rules are implemented by the government on behalf of private parties who in turn support the politician that promises to enact the rules. This is an anti-biblical corruption, a form of crony capitalism, and a common means by which the rich oppress the poor today. Examples of these rules include compulsory union membership, excessive professional and business licensing, and regulated monopolies with corrupt regulation. Many redevelopment agencies and "private-public partnerships" involve the government picking economic winners with political money changing hands behind the scenes.

6. The whole system of **civil justice** has largely degenerated into a monopoly money-making scheme for the members of the legal establishment which operates, like most unions, for the benefit of its members. The practice of law is limited to members. All judges are members, as are most legislators. To complete the circle, trial lawyers are often the principle contributors to the political campaigns of their fellow lawyer judges and politicians. The whole system is operated nominally for the benefit of society but actually for the benefit of the members. Class action law has been developed to allow lawyers to get richer than most industrialists, owning sports teams and at least one major political party. The cost of lawsuit abuse is passed on to the poor consumer on whose behalf the trial lawyers claim to work. Any attempt to change our economic system to comport with scripture will have to include tort reform as a major component.

7. Various corporate forms of doing business include a **limitation of liability**. The liability of the owners is normally limited to the amount of their investment. If Joe does business as Joe's

Hotdog Stand, Joe is liable for all business debt and his personal assets and future income may be reached to satisfy those debts. If he does business as Joe's Hotdog Stand, Inc., his personal assets are protected. The liability for his actions, however, does not just go away. It is absorbed by society at large in the person of his various creditors. The limited liability forms of doing business involve the creation by the government of a fictitious person, a corporation, which is given this liability protection by the government. All such corporations therefore have their creator, the government, as a silent partner. They are neither truly private nor truly public entities. Unlike a real person, they have neither a body to beat nor a soul to damn. To a large degree they separate ownership from responsibility and are a hybrid between a private enterprise and socialism. The owners, which is to say stockholders, tend to act like absentee landlords, caring little for how the business is run as long as they get their earnings. Artificial liability limitation creates what is known as a "moral hazard" in which the borrower gets to enjoy the advantages of a risk while others shoulder the risk. This encourages the owners to take on more debt than a fully liable owner prudently would. This arrangement is thus also contrary to the biblical principle of limiting societal indebtedness. The reason government favors the corporate form of business is precisely to gain undue influence over business as an instrument of social control.

8. **Private property** is to be protected. Biblical law required indebted land to return to its hereditary owners periodically whether the debt had been paid or not. In addition to preventing a stratified society of creditors and debtors, it indicates a desire to have people identify with their land in some sense which we have today lost. Inheritance tax often acts to prevent families from passing property on to heirs. Eminent domain and other "takings" abuse also work against this principle. Modern government seeks to own all property and reduce the citizenry to slave-like renters.

A further discussion of economics is contained in Appendix E.

INTERNATIONAL RELATIONS

After the flood we are told that mankind, speaking one common language, traveled eastward[26] to the plains of Shinar, where they built the tower of Babel in an effort to remain united under the centralized rule of Nimrod.[27] God, however, frowned on this effort and scattered them into the various nations by confusing their languages. This resulted in a suboptimal situation where the many small nations frequently war with each other and have only limited trade relationships. God did this because the alternative, given man's unredeemed and rebellious state, was a global tyranny of unlimited evil that would stand in the way of his plan of redemption.

We have seen how a succession of empires arose that sought to reunite mankind under similar systems of global empire. The book of Revelation speaks of a man called the "beast" who would likewise establish an anti-Christian world empire. In our day, there have been many attempts to create trans-national political unions, including the League of Nations, the United Nations, the European Union, and others. These have all rightly been seen by Christians as embodying the same anti-Christian imperial spirit as their predecessors. All of these have been particularly hostile to biblical Christianity which they see as divisive of mankind's unity. The unity of mankind they seek is just man's common rebellion against God, expressed in a diversity of ways. The one thing radical Moslems, atheists, racists, militant homosexuals, materialistic businessmen, corrupt politicians, and apostate Christians agree on is that they do not want to acknowledge the law of God or their need for the gospel of Jesus Christ. As we are told in the second psalm, the kings of the earth rise up and their rulers take council together against the Lord and his anointed. Beyond this, they may disagree and fight about everything else as each seeks to go his own anarchistic way.

Tyrannical empires dream of uniting mankind by force and creating an anti-Christian, humanistic utopia. God, however, will frustrate all such plans. World peace will come, to the extent it does come, in this present age, from the triumph of the Christian Empire as it converts men and

---

26. In the Bible, eastward movement often symbolizes apostasy.
27. Genesis 10:9-10

reforms governments in all nations. Complete world peace will only be ushered in after the Second Coming of Christ.

Standing in opposition to human schemes of the world empire is "the stone cut without hands." As a matter of historical fact, Christ has come, bringing joy to those who have longed for his appearing and horror to his enemies. His coming has destroyed in principle this whole mad dream of man concluding a successful rebellion by setting up a global humanistic empire and has also destroyed it in fact. For even as sinners concoct one new world order scheme after another, God blows on it from heaven, subjecting it to futility. Meanwhile, the Empire of the Lord Jesus Christ continues to grow and advance. The gospel message continues to be spread like sown seed, finding hearts of diverse quality, yielding differing fruit, but spreading and growing nonetheless. The stone grows to become a mountain that will fill the whole earth, a mountain to which all nations flow and to which the kings of the earth bring their glory.

All humanistic would-be empires are based on lies and the principle of top-down application of force. The Empire of the Son of God is based on truth and the principle of bottom-up conversion of souls and minds. As it grows and fills the hearts of more and more people, nations are affected and changed. A nation cannot be "Christian" in the same sense that an individual can be Christian. Collective entities like nations and institutions can only be "Christianized." That is, they can have their structures, policies, and cultures brought into conformity with the law of God and the gospel of Jesus Christ. Justice rather than favoritism can rule in their courts. Unjust practices like slavery and abortion can be outlawed. Immoral and destructive behavior can be suppressed. Peaceful relations can be established among Christianized nations.

The idea that the law of God can be known to a large extent by reason and observation even without the Bible is the basis of Natural Law theory. A similar concept known as the Law of Nations exists, which can be thought of as Natural Law scaled up to control international relations.

The principal alternative to Natural Law is the idea of Legal Positivism. Where Natural Law considers law as preexisting, and God given, Legal Positivism denies the existence of God and his law and holds that the only law which exists or can exist is that which is made by man in a "positive" act, such as legislation or judicial fiat. In the same way, the alternative to the Law of Nations is the modern idea of International Law, a legal positivist idea of laws made by treaties or international bodies like the United Nations. Christians should champion the idea of Natural Law over Legal Positivism and the Law of Nations over International Law.

A Christian (or Christianized) nation will consider itself bound to relate to other nations in terms of the Law of Nations rather than to International Law. International Law will typically be anti-Christian in character. It may coincide with the Law of Nations on any particular instance, or it may not. For example, Iraq's invasion of Kuwait could have been seen as a violation of both the Law of Nations and International Law, while some international court's ruling that Israel had no right to respond to terrorist attacks might put International Law and the Law of Nations in conflict.

As a Christian nation, how should the United States relate to other nations? We should relate to them the same way a Christian individual should relate to their fellow man. We should love our neighbor as ourselves and do unto other nations as we would have them do unto us. We would treat all nations justly in terms of God's moral law and not take undue advantage of our greater strength. But we would also make distinctions between nations that are more Christian and lawful and those that are not. We would not have to pretend that all cultures are equal any more than we do in our private lives. We should not allow ourselves to be unequally yoked.

The United Nations along with many other world bodies are not organized along these lines. It pretends that lawful republics, dictatorships, and mass murdering hell-holes are all the same. This leads to a ridiculous situation where we are paying dues to be members of a club where most of the members wish us and our friends ill. The United States could still belong and make some use of it but would have to recognize its true character and treat it more as a debating forum and sometimes useful tool rather than as a first step toward some kind of antichrist world government. A far better solution would be to degrade our support and membership and start another international organization of more lawful and legitimate governments.

A Christian nation should be seeking to advance the kingdom of God on earth. To do this, it should form its most important alliances with like-minded countries. One idea might be a "League of Lawful Nations," consisting of nations that affirm and act in accordance with some public formulation of the Law of Nations. This would exclude what we today sometimes call "rogue states" like North Korea, Iran, and Cuba.

FREE SPEECH

Free speech is a myth. Free speech is certainly not an aspect of biblical law where blasphemy and urging the worship of other gods were capital offenses. No society that seeks continued existence can tolerate speech that attacks its very foundations. Certainly, liberals who claim to champion free speech have zero tolerance for any speech that goes against the humanistic order they are seeking to establish and enforce this zero tolerance to the extent they have power to do so. Like little ivy-covered North Koreas, nearly all college campuses are controlled by liberals and have rigorously enforced speech codes. College administrators allow left wing brown shirts to shout down and even assault conservative speakers with impunity. They also champion "hate speech" laws which criminalize any disagreement with their policy preferences. In interpreting the first amendment they insist that it protects pornography and prohibits prayer. While the theory is that toleration of anti-Christian speech should enlarge freedom for pro-Christian speech, all experience is to the contrary.

From colonial days until the latter part of the twentieth century, America criminalized and censored pornography, foul speech, and blasphemy. Recent toleration of these assaults on our foundations reflects not confidence and strength, but insecurity and weakness. Only a people alienated from their own roots would tolerate such things. This is all the more so when the targets of this destructive speech are the children of Christian homes, which Christ's enemies seek to corrupt and destroy. God will hold their parents and pastors accountable for failing to defend them.

There must indeed be tolerance for tolerable opinions, but there must also be limits. If our fathers saw us shrug it off when men curse

God and burn our flag in public, they would disown us. Censorship and limits on foul and blasphemous speech must be restored.

Biblical Law and Freedom

Rebellious man sees God's law as oppression. The redeemed see it for what it is: the condition for our life. The law of God is to man what water is to a fish. A fish may want to get out of his tank and frolic on the carpet, but if he succeeds in this endeavor he will find only death. In the same way man may chafe at the restrictions of biblical morality and seek freedom in rebellion and lawlessness, but his fate will be no different from that of the fish.[28] Man does not live by bread alone, but by every word that proceeds from the mouth of God. As God's creature, man finds his greatest satisfaction and indeed his greatest freedom when he aligns his life with the law of his maker. The same is true for a nation that seeks to make its laws conform to the divine precepts. Such a legal system will grant man the maximum degree of freedom that is truly possible. Would-be tyrants offer the people a false freedom from responsible behavior in the sexual, moral, and financial areas. In exchange, the people grant the tyrant similar freedom to rule over them without restraint. It is the devil's bargain.

Discussion Questions

1. How and to what extent should we use Old Testament law in forming our modern laws?

2. Should a modern Christianized nation permit the practice of non-Christian religions? If so, to what extent?

3. Should capital punishment be part of a modern Christian order? Should it be used for all the crimes for which it was used in the Old Testament? Why or why not?

4. Under biblical law, land was kept in the family and passed down to the eldest son. It could not even be sold or given away permanently. How would you apply this principle today?

---

28. Job 36:13-14

PART IV:

HOT TOPICS

What would it mean for the Church to move in the spirit and power of Elijah? John the Baptist (who according to Jesus was Elijah[29]) rebuked Herod concerning the wife of his brother Phillip, saying, "It is not lawful for you to have her." Here was an itinerant prophet, clothed in camel hair, calling the great king to account in terms of God's law. Such is the role of the prophet. Even so, the church must begin confronting civil authority with the law of God. Government officials today believe that they are independent of God in heaven and are answerable to their political power base alone. Why should they not believe this when God's prophets are unwilling to call them on it?

It is of no concern whether the church can muster enough votes to make these public officials tremble. That is God's role. When Paul appeared before Felix (in chains) and reasoned with him about righteousness, temperance, and judgment to come, Felix trembled. The Holy Spirit has been sent into the world to reprove the world of sin, and righteousness, and judgment to come. God may vindicate his Word by political change, by striking his enemies dead, by changing their minds and bringing them to repentance, or by any number of other means. That is his part. It is the role of the church to faithfully and boldly preach the Word.

---

29. Matthew 11:14

If I profess with the loudest voice and clearest exposition every portion of the truth of God except precisely that little point which the world and the devil are at that moment attacking, I am not confessing Christ, however boldly I may be professing Christ. Where the battle rages, there the loyalty of the soldier is proved; and to be steady on all the battlefield besides, is mere flight and disgrace if he flinches at that point. (Martin Luther, 1483-1546)

It is the role of the church to speak the whole counsel of God to the surrounding culture, including the governing authorities. The church can and should speak to all of the issues of the day. However, there are four especially critical issues where the need for this ministry is acute, because these are the exact points which the world and the devil are currently attacking, as evidenced by the fierce reaction to the preaching of God's Word concerning them. They are also issues where the strong are unjustly harming the weak. The church must boldly proclaim God's Word on these specific matters or risk being cast out and trodden under the feet of men. These four issues are (1) abortion, (2) the homosexual political agenda, (3) Christian persecution, and (4) education.

ABORTION

Abortion is man's most direct challenge to God's law today. The original institution of civil government in Genesis 9:6 established capital punishment for anyone who destroyed innocent human life. For civil government to deny this protection to any class of innocent human beings is the most direct challenge to God's law imaginable. To do the worst thing possible to the most innocent people in the world is the apex of antinomianism and rebellion.

Abortion is an evil so horrific that it cannot be appreciated by words alone. The use of graphic pictures of abortion is a necessary part of any effort to outlaw it.[30] Illegal activity and especially violence to oppose abortion is unnecessary and counterproductive. It amounts to a capitulation to the very spirit of lawlessness that lies behind abortion. Unpopular activity to expose the reality of abortion and expose the role of various public figures in support of it is absolutely necessary.

---

30. See abortionNO.org.

For the church to remain virtually silent on this is contemptible cowardice. Why would anyone pay attention to anything the church has to say if it will not take a principled stand at this point?

Many pastors and other leaders who theoretically oppose legal abortion place the issue on the back burner by directing Christian activity to other worthy but less critical matters. To use the words of Martin Luther, they are willing to oppose the devil anywhere on the battle line except where he is currently attacking. Such leaders are functionally supporting legalized abortion and should be called on it. The failure of the church to make anything other than the most tepid response to this horror undermines any claim on her part to be speaking for God and destroys her evangelistic witness in the world.

THE HOMOSEXUAL POLITICAL AGENDA

Dealing with individuals concerning their struggles with homosexual tendencies is one thing; dealing with the public homosexual political agenda is something else. The sin of homosexual acts is not inherently worse than any other sin, but because our sexuality is so deeply part of our identity, its effects can run very deep. Since it is strongly reinforced by habit, freedom and change, while achievable, can be more difficult than other sins.

The homosexual political agenda goes far beyond concern for persons involved in homosexual activity. The agenda is aimed at silencing the witness of the faithful church. It begins by defining persons who engage in homosexual behavior as having an unchangeable "orientation" genetically fixed at birth. There is no scientific evidence for this "gay gene," or for that matter, the idea that any behavior is genetically determined. The construct is political, not scientific. By framing the argument in this manner, proponents of the homosexual political agenda are able to equate opposition to homosexual behavior with racism, co-opt the successful civil rights movement, and marginalize their opponents. If the church accepts the homosexual political agenda it compromises the Word of God and loses its only power. If the church opposes the agenda, she is marginalized as "hateful" and "homophobic." Either way, her power in society is reduced. This is why the homosexual political agenda is supported by so many antinomians,[31] even those that hate homosexuals. Silencing the church is job one.

Biblically, homosexual behavior, not tendencies, is the issue. God ordained sex for a man and a woman in marriage with a view toward procreation. Homosexual acts, like other sexual sins, are transgressions of God's law. Man's law must be made to conform to the law of God. Therefore, male homosexual acts, even between consenting adults in private, must be illegal. No compromise position such as civil unions is possible, nor will homosexual political activists ever settle for such a compromise.

Most of the homosexual political agenda is targeted at children and young adults and is therefore predatory. The public school is for the most part under their control, with indoctrination into their storyline permeating normal subjects such as reading, writing, and arithmetic. Many high schools and junior high schools have so-called Gay-Straight Alliance clubs, ostensibly to reduce bullying of gay students but actually there to groom troubled and vulnerable children for homosexual activity. Such clubs allow students involved in homosexual relationships to recruit other confused and troubled young people into experimental relationships after school, possibly at one of their adult friend's apartment. The clubs may thus function as fishing holes for local pedophiles. School board members know this and either think this is a good thing or do not care.

Efforts to force the Boy Scouts to join the Girl Scouts in promoting acceptance of homosexual behavior have recently succeeded. Placing children from troubled families into the custody of unrelated adults in homosexual relationships makes judges feel righteous. Recent changes to the law to encourage open homosexual relationships in the military are part of this same pattern. The assertion that the homosexual political agenda has nothing to do with pedophilia is suspect at the very least. The notion that the homosexual political agenda is one of "live and let live" is hopelessly naive.

Pastors are charged by God to look out for the welfare of the young of their flocks. Few pastors have lifted a finger or said a word to stop this destruction of the children under their care by the local school boards. Many pastors are worried that if the homosexual political agenda goes further, the government might shut down their church for "hate

---

31. Opponents of God's law.

speech." If these same pastors are unwilling to stand up for the young of their flocks, perhaps they should be shut down.

The destructive nature of the homosexual political agenda has reached its height with the Supreme Court's supposed discovery of a Constitutional mandate for the oxymoron of "same-sex marriage." Aristotle said, "It was the worst form of inequality to try to make unequal things equal." Whatever same-sex couples do, it is not marriage. Calling it marriage destroys the institution of marriage the same way counterfeit money destroys real money. It makes the honorable institution of holy matrimony a joke, thereby destroying marriage and the family altogether, and as the institution of the family recedes, the institution of the government takes over.

We should note that this has not happened as suddenly as people think. Our society has been steadily devaluing marriage with pornography, toleration of cohabitation, "palimony," and no-fault divorce. One reason many people say "why not?" to same-sex marriage is because marriage is a legal nothing. How can we be so mean as to deny homosexuals a thing of zero value?

Homosexual acts are contrary to the design purpose of God which is evident in nature and explicit in scripture. This design purpose is to provide for the continuity of society. The sanctity of the sexual relationship between a man and his wife in marriage is the foundation of the family, and the family is the cellular unit of society. De-sanctifying marriage destroys the family and subverts social order, on which we all depend. Standing against this aspect of the homosexual political agenda is imperative.

Jesus taught on marriage as a man-woman union specifically.[32] Christians who are ashamed of Jesus and his words in the midst of this adulterous and sinful generation will find Jesus ashamed of them when he comes in the glory of his Father with the holy angels.[33]

CHRISTIAN PERSECUTION

When one member of the body suffers, all suffer with it. Today, Christians in other parts of the world suffer a great or greater persecution

32. Matthew 19:4-6
33. Mark 8:38

than they ever have. The church in America is nearly silent and has never made the relief of their suffering brethren a matter of much concern. Even when Christians in America suffer lesser persecutions, church leaders are largely silent.

David was a model shepherd. When a lion or a bear would attack one of the sheep under his care, he would attack the animal, seize it, and strike it dead. In contrast, when individual Christians are under attack today, whether in the school system, the work place, or the courts, the last people you see rising to their defense are the local pastors. The job of defending persecuted Christians is outsourced to various para- church ministries.

Local churches must band together and stand up for their freedom and the freedom of their members to live godly lives. The church in America must stand with their persecuted brethren overseas. Support—financial, moral, and spiritual—should be provided to them. Letter writing campaigns to elected officials, the US State Department, and the leaders of other nations, protesting the mistreatment of Christians, should be organized and become a routine activity. If the church saw herself as engaged in the spiritual battle of the ages, rather than as engaged in religious social gatherings, this sort of activity in support of the persecuted church might seem more natural.

In recent days we have seen open government persecution of individual Christians who are unwilling to participate in the sins of others by paying for abortions, or participating in the desecration of marriage, or even speaking out on moral issues. Might this be a result of our failure to stand with our brothers who are being murdered for their faith in other countries? Either way, it is past time for us to stand together.

EDUCATION

God has given parents the responsibility to oversee the education and training of their children. They are to "train up" their children in the way they should go.[34] Government schools since the time of Horace Mann have been dedicated to de-Christianizing the children from Christian homes, robbing them of their faith and morals, and driving a wedge between them and their parents. Today the situation has become

34. Proverbs 22:6

extreme, with overt brain washing, political indoctrination, and gay sex clubs. The state asserts total control over *its* children, distaining any role for parents except for paying the bills.

Removing Christian children from state schools and providing them with godly education has become imperative. Parents must do this and the churches must assist them. Providing Christian schools is more important than providing luxury church buildings and ego monuments. If this is not done, the church in America may not survive. Again, pastors must take the lead.

The book of Acts records a time when the church in Jerusalem pulled together, with people selling their property and placing the proceeds at the apostles' feet, so that there was no needy person among them. It may take sacrifices like that for the church to save her next generation. Or perhaps a fraction of that effort in the political sphere would yield the same result.

PART V:

THE FUTURE AND THE END

OUR PRESENT STATE

Each of the last three major periods of history, the Renaissance, the Reformation, and Enlightenment, lasted about 250 years. The Renaissance lasted from about 1250 to 1500 AD, the Reformation from 1500 to 1750 AD, and the Enlightenment, or modern era, from 1750 to the present. It is almost as if it takes about that long for a major organizing idea to exhaust itself as men try all of its variations. We seem to be at the end of this highly humanistic period that began with the French Revolution, moved on to fascism and communism, and is ending with some kind of liberal commercialism. The early phases of this period were marked by passionate enthusiasm for the various ideologies which each acted as a substitute religion. Today no one believes in fascism or communism, and liberal consumerism, a purely hedonistic and materialistic denial of meaning, also appears to be undergoing collapse with the disintegration of the European Union among other developments.

The end of this Enlightenment era will be characterized by great anxiety and turmoil as all of the old verities collapse. Europe, being the center of the Enlightenment project, is a dead man walking. Unwilling to even biologically reproduce and concerned only with a moderately comfortable ride to the grave, Europeans seem resigned to importing Islamic laborers and leaving their countries to them. Resurgent Islam indeed looks vital in comparison to dying Europe, but this is an illusion. Islam is in a terminal crisis of its own.

Radical Islam with its jihad, terrorism and extreme Sharia Law is a reaction to its confrontation with modernity to which it cannot adapt. Islam grows only by its relatively high birth rates, not by conversion. Those birth rates, by the way, while higher than that of Europe, are still below replacement rates.[35] Its appeal is defensive, an understandable attempt to prevent the atheism and sexual immorality of the decadent west from sweeping it away. Islam, however, lacks intellectual vitality and offers no positive vision. Islamic nations, for the most part, produce little of commercial value and would be utterly impoverished were it not for oil. Jihad and terrorism are not the tools of a conquering army. They are the desperate acts of the doomed, reminiscent of the post–Civil War Ku Klux Klan fighting for a lost cause. While Western secularism and Islam seem to be polar opposites, they actually have much in common. Both are in love with death, both embrace irrationality, and both are essentially Christian heresies on steroids. They sprang from Christian cultures, borrowed from Christianity heavily, and are united in their war against Christ.

Christianity is, in the final analysis, the only game in town. Only the Christian faith affirms life and offers meaning. Christianity is the fastest growing religion in the world. This is either in spite of or because of a level of persecution that rivals the worst days of the old Roman Empire. In communist and Muslim countries, the persecution is horrific. Rape, torture, imprisonment, confiscation of property, and murder are normal fare for Christians in these countries. The West, led by secularists and compromised Christians, cares very little about the mistreatment of Christians abroad and adds its own low level persecution of them at home. Even so, as the only faith offering people hope in troubled times, it continues to grow. Though it suffers persecution on a massive scale, it continues inexorably to take over the world.

"BUT I THOUGHT JESUS WAS COMING TO TAKE US AWAY?"

When Jesus was about to ascend into heaven, the disciples asked him when he was going to restore the kingdom to Israel. He answered

---

35. See *How Civilizations Die: (And Why Islam is Dying Too)* by David Goldman.

that it was not for them to know such things. Rather, they were to follow orders, go to Jerusalem, receive the empowering of the Holy Spirit, and be his witnesses to the uttermost parts of the earth. He wanted them to be about the business of advancing the kingdom. They wanted to speculate on the timing of end time events.

Many modern Christians sound like those disciples at Christ's ascension. Prophecy books and seminars are popular as eager Christians listen to earnest teachers speculate about how some newspaper headline fulfills some prophecy about the antichrist. What is forgotten in all of this is that the book of Revelation is properly called, "The Revelation of Jesus Christ," not, "The Revelation of the Antichrist." The term *antichrist* is not even mentioned in the book of Revelation.

Christians today do not know and are not supposed to know the exact time and manner in which God in his wisdom is going to bring about the culmination of all things. What his servants should care about is doing the work to which they are called. Christians should be about advancing and enjoying the kingdom of God on earth. While they eagerly look for his coming, like servants who do not know when their master will return, they should be anxious to be found busy in his work when he does return. If we make this our rule of life, we will not have to correctly guess the time of his coming. The church will always be ready.

Versions of eschatology[36] which tend to weaken the hands of the saints for the work are a major problem. However the end times are going to unfold in the providence of God, the church should have the attitude of a conquering army that expects to win. If her eschatology causes her to sin by adopting a weak, pessimistic, loser mindset and hence shrinking from the battle, she should cut that eschatology off and cast it aside.

The right way to look at the prophecies in the book of Revelation is to see them as having multiple fulfillments or applications. They speak to the church under Jewish and Roman persecution in the first centuries, to believers in the middle ages, to Christians in the present time, and will speak to the church in the end times whenever that may be. The pattern we see in the prophecies is the same as we see in church history: a struggling, persecuted but faithful church that always seems to be losing but which in fact is always winning, and which

---

36. Beliefs concerning the end times.

is destined to triumph. **The book of Revelation is a worship and warfare manual for the church, relevant in every century**. Would the church not be more powerful and effective if it was collectively praying its way repeatedly through "The Revelation of Jesus Christ," applying its themes to the battles it was in, rather than arguing over who the antichrist was or is going to be? At least the members of the body of Christ would be battling the world system rather than arguing with each other over speculative matters. That might even have the benefit of hastening the coming of the Lord.

WARFARE WORSHIP

The church on earth is called the *Church Militant,* and the church in heaven is called the *Church Triumphant.* The book of Revelation shows us how the worship of the whole church governs the world.[37] The prayers of the earthbound saints assembled in corporate worship go up like incense to the throne room of God in heaven, where the saints in heaven and all the heavenly hosts are likewise gathered in worship. In response to these prayers, lightning and thunders and a great earthquake are poured out on earth. In other words, when the Church Militant, assembled in its official capacity, joins with the Church Triumphant in worshiping God and bringing prayers and supplications to his throne, God moves in power on the earth and changes the course of history.

In contrast, worship in churches today looks nothing like this at all. The idea that the church worships to wage war, change history, and advance the kingdom against its foes is almost completely absent everywhere. If worship is not dead liturgy, it is vapid Christian entertainment. At best, it is a "bless me and pray for you" service. The idea that the church gathers together to wage war in worship is alien. This is why the church lacks power, and why, despite her numbers, wealth, and programs, she is losing the cultural battle to her much weaker foes. When reformation in worship along the lines of "The Revelation of Jesus Christ" begins, that will be reformation that matters.

---

37. Revelation 8:3-5

PREDICTIONS

The natural trend of fallen man is always the same. It is a trend toward a slave society ruled over by an antichrist man-god, like Hitler or Pharaoh or Caesar. It is a straight line to widespread anarchy culminating in tyranny, poverty, bloodshed, and spiritual darkness, all of which is but a prelude to hell and eternal damnation. It is easy therefore to look at trends and predict doom and gloom. The only reason there is anything in history besides doom and gloom is because of God's unfolding plan of salvation, and the only institution on earth that makes a difference is the church, the body of Christ.

The ultimate triumph of Christ's kingdom on earth and in history is guaranteed by Christ himself, seated at the right hand of God, angels, powers, and principalities being made subject to him. The believer need not be worried about this ultimate outcome. The believer should, however, be very worried about what part his life or his generation will play in the total picture. Will it be one of the highlights or lowlights? Will the believer sit at the head table or near the kitchen at the marriage supper of the Lamb? Therefore, just as the Christian looks for the hand of God in history, in anticipating the future he looks for what God is doing. The most important trend to look for is what the Holy Spirit is doing in the church. The rest is secondary at best.

Two powerful moves of the Holy Spirit have been progressing in this generation. They can be seen in parts of the church that are showing vitality. These are about to merge into something of irresistible force on the earth.

The first of these moves is the outpouring of the Spirit in the Pentecostal and Charismatic movements. The reactivation of long dormant spiritual gifts in the church is one of the greatest untold stories of this generation. Especially in the poorest parts of the world, but also in the richest and everywhere in between, and in every denomination, believers are rediscovering the Baptism with the Holy Spirit, tongues, healings, and the working of miracles. This is the *Revivalist* stream.[38]

The second move has been on the intellectual front. The Christian mind is breaking free of both the oppression of humanistic intellectual intimidation and the crippling effects of its own synthesis with pagan thought.

---

38. See *Megashift* by James H. Rutz.

The intellectual defense of the Christian faith has been strengthened by the emergence of presuppositional apologetics, a renewed readiness to defend the Genesis account of origins and the authority of the Bible in general, and the application of biblical truth in practical political battles especially over abortion and sexual morality. Under such labels as Dominionism, Theonomy, and Reconstructionism, Christian thinkers have been advancing a much more uncompromised and uncompromising assertion of God's authority over all matters. Similar vitality is seen in many segments of the Roman Catholic Church, which often is forced to take the brunt of the public battle with the enemies of Christ. This is the *Reformist* stream.

These two streams seem completely different and even antagonistic. The Pentecostal and Charismatic wing of Revivalists tends to be anti-intellectual and escapist. The Christian Reconstruction wing of Reformers is hyper-intellectual and suspicious of the experiential slain-in-the-spirit, talking-in-tongues, funny-doctrine-prone Charismatics. But these two streams are already beginning to flow together.

In the Bible, the signs and wonders always are associated with confirming the Word. The signs and wonders–focused Revivalists are sloppy about the Word. Reformers are uncomfortable with the emotionalism of Pentecost. But in the Bible, the Word and the Spirit always go together.

And they went forth, and preached everywhere, the Lord working with them, confirming the word *with* signs *following. Amen. (Mark 16:20)*

And now Lord, behold their threatenings, and grant unto thy servants that with all boldness they may speak thy word, *by stretching forth thine hand to heal, and that* signs and wonders *may be done by the name of thy holy child Jesus. (Acts 4:29-30)*

And now, behold, the hand of the Lord is upon thee, and thou shalt be blind, not seeing the sun for a season. And immediately there fell on him a mist and a darkness, and he went about seeking some to lead him by the hand. Then the deputy, when he saw what was done, *believed, being astonished at the* doctrine *of the Lord. (Acts 13:11-12)*

For the kingdom of God is not in word *[only], but in* power. *(1 Corinthians 4:20)*

The Word comes first. Signs follow to confirm the Word. Revivalists will see a lot more signs when they get serious about the Word. Revivalists are in danger of drifting into all kinds of errors and heresies if they do not drop the anti-intellectual posture and become students of the Word, workmen who do not need to be ashamed. They also fail to equip the next generation with the knowledge of the truth they will need to withstand attacks on the faith from secular schools and religious heretics.

The preaching of the Word, however, does not achieve victory through intellectual or rhetorical brilliance, nor by any other human artifice, but by the demonstration of the Spirit and of power. Reformers need to recognize their need for the Holy Spirit's power. Conferences, newsletters, websites, political action, and scholarship are all necessary, but not sufficient. Human intellectual pride must yield to the Bible's command to receive the supernatural empowerment of the Holy Spirit.

What is going to make these two movements flow together? It is already happening. The lack of revival in the Revivalist churches and the inability of the Reformer churches to effect societal reformation and the resulting persecution is driving both to their knees. From there, God is leading each to the other. Furthermore, as the larger society has become more hostile to Christ and Christians, shared persecution is forcing the two camps together. Many have already met outside of abortion clinics and inside of courtrooms and jails.

There is a third group that is going to join these two. Many non-religious and non-Christian conservative groups are unaware of just what it is they are trying to conserve. The features of the American system they find so attractive originated in this nation's Christian foundations. How can the individual claim any importance against the great collective? It is only the Christian faith that gives the reason why the individual is of so great importance. Each individual is going to live forever, either in heaven or hell. No collective state can say that about itself. Only Christianity places such infinite worth on the individual and the importance of his conscience before God. All must fear encroaching on the relationship of the individual to the true and living God. This and this alone is the basis for freedom. The time is coming when non-religious conservatives are going to have to face this fact. Republicans are going to have their own "come to Jesus" moment very soon.

America still has a large and serious Christian population. Their loss of power has not been due so much to a loss of faith, as in Europe, but due to a false dualistic doctrine with its inadequate confession of Christ's lordship. Many American Christians are taught to be very passive about government, to stay out of politics, and to accept the decline of their culture as part of the end times prophesized in Revelation. Others care deeply about the future of their country, their children, and grandchildren. They know they should be involved but don't know how.

The shock of watching American liberties suddenly lost, and the sudden rise of Christian persecution, may be just what the church in America needs to wake up. The success of the militant gay rights movement in getting homosexual activity enshrined as a civil right that trumps religious freedom, freedom of speech, and freedom of association has led to a legal situation where Bible believing Christians are now considered the same as racists. Already the public schools near-universally consider it their duty to indoctrinate Christian children to this effect. Do Christians want to see their own children reporting them to the authorities for "hate speech?" Do they want to see public child welfare advocates appointed to visit their homes and supervise their parenting? Do they want to see even more children removed from their Christian homes and assigned to homosexual couples for proper instruction in these matters? If Christians resist these things, they will be listed as "hate group members," demonized in the media, and penalized with respect to employment, tax exemption, and zoning variances. They will be ostracized by friends and family. Many pastors, already skilled at compromising, will, in the face of this pressure and under the influence of the implicit polytheism of "separation of church and state," compromise further, becoming like the officially recognized "patriotic churches" in China. Some are there already.

If Christians must experience these things, it will be the judgment of God on a church whose salt has lost its savor; on an escapist church instead of a Church Militant. Dualism is an error that effectively denies the total lordship of Jesus Christ. All of this will be a separation of the wheat from the chaff. His fan is in his hand.[39]

Far from being post-Christian, the world is still very much pre-Christian. The church still has much work to do to fulfill the Great Commission and extend the Empire of her Lord over all the nations of mankind. The Christian's job is not finished when they get people to make an initial profession of faith or join the local church. Christ's disciples are to make disciples of all nations and take every thought captive to the obedience of Christ. The knowledge of God is to cover the earth as the waters cover the sea. Let he who has ears hear what the Spirit is saying to the church.

CONCLUSION

The church of Jesus Christ will most assuredly survive and conquer. That is not even a question. The question is, will the church of this generation contribute to this victory or be an embarrassing footnote in history? Today, the vast majority of the church in the Western world is either in the conformist or escapist camp and headed for the embarrassing footnote. The ranks of the Church Militant are thin. Yet there are hopeful signs of life. Many are praying and fasting for revival. Others are laboring in the Word and fighting for the truth and reformation. Some are even willing to get their hands dirty in the political trenches. Furthermore, the competing anti-Christian systems, although currently riding high, seem headed for imminent collapse through debt, infertility, and intellectual vacuity, if not outright insanity. The immediate future therefore remains very much in doubt.

Jesus did not commission his church to conform to the culture of the world, and he did not commission her to hide from the world awaiting his return. He commissioned her to make disciples of all nations; to teach them to obey all of his commandments. In short, he commissioned her to conquer the world. He is that stone cut without hands, and his people are that growing mountain that is to fill the earth.

Again the Christian conquest of the world is not to be pursued like the Islamic conquest of the world, with fire and sword. It is

---

39. Matthew 3:12; Luke 3:17

accomplished by the preaching of the Word and with the demonstration of the Spirit's power; it is a bottom-up conversion of individuals, leading to a reformation of society along the lines of biblical law and justice.

For too long Christians have vacillated between conformity and escape. How many have suffered; how many have perished without Christ because of this failure to act in accordance with the Lord's commission? How long has the church allowed the lies of the enemy to lead her off the path? The time has come for her to shake off slumber and to free herself from the heresy of Christ's limited lordship. The time has come for the bride of Christ to assume her place of rule by his side. The Spirit and the Bride say, "come." What an eternal tragedy it would be to miss God's calling in this day of his strong moving because of fear, self-love, some religious error, or majoring on minor issues. That would give a new meaning to "left behind."

DISCUSSION QUESTIONS

1. How do the many historic denominations figure into this picture of the church as being in three real groups of conformists, escapists, and militants?

2. Can you identify other significant modern moves of the Holy Spirit besides those mentioned in this chapter?

3. How would you change your church's order of worship to orient it to spiritual warfare and the government of the world?

4. How might you reorder your life to make sure you were part of the Church Militant?

Appendix A:
Salvation

For whosoever shall call upon the name of the Lord shall be saved.
(Romans 10:13)

Our Need for Salvation

...that through death he (Jesus) might destroy him that had the power of death, that is, the devil; and deliver them who through fear of death were all their lifetime subject to bondage. (Hebrews 2:14-15)

The fact of death hangs over all of us from birth. Death involves fear, fear of the end of everything one has known, the end of all hopes and dreams, and the fear of what comes next. This unresolved issue of death burdens all of life, placing us in mental bondage such that we are not free to just live our lives.

And as it is appointed unto men once to die, but after this the judgment. (Hebrews 9:27)

Guilt over things we have done and things we have left undone is our common burden. We feel guilty because we are guilty. The sense that our lives would not stand up to any final judgment by our Maker is universal. As a result, man does many things to free himself from this guilt and fear. He may try very hard to be a "good person," or to achieve some great thing, or to follow some strict regimen of religious practice. Alternatively, he may give himself over to rebellion, sin, and a "devil may care" attitude; a false bravado and a whistling past the graveyard. Seldom does any of this work. At best it may provide a distraction or give some vague hope that one has been "good enough to get in."

WE CANNOT SAVE OURSELVES

But we are all as an unclean thing, and all our righteousness is as filthy rags... (Isaiah 64:6)

Try as we might to convince ourselves of our righteousness, we are never fooled. We all know that we fall short. We try and convince ourselves by saying, "at least I'm better than that other guy," but we somehow know that God is not going to grade on a curve. We know that we do not even live up to our own standards, let alone God's, and even our best deeds are contaminated by impure motives. In the end we are left with this stark fact: there is nothing we can do to further our chances of getting into heaven.

GOD'S FREE GIFT

And they were astonished out of measure, saying among themselves, Who then can be saved? And Jesus looking upon them saith, With men it is impossible, but not with God: for with God all things are possible. (Mark 10:26-27)

It is precisely when we are at the end of our ability that God acts. What is impossible with men is possible with God. We cannot make ourselves right with God by anything we do, but God has made a way through the sacrifice of Jesus Christ. He is the Lamb of God that takes away the sin of the world. As the only innocent man to ever live, he takes upon himself the sin of the world, and in particular the sin of those who come to him in repentance and belief, paying the just penalty for their sin in his own body on the cross, and making them just as if they had never sinned. The blood of Jesus washes white as snow. Salvation is a free gift of God. You just have to receive it.

RECEIVING SALVATION

Receiving this free gift is not as easy as it sounds. There are two serious mental barriers. The first is your willingness to humble yourself enough to admit both your need of salvation and your inability to earn it, the second to believe that this good news is true. Mere intellectual assent is not enough. It is not enough to believe that the high wire artist can push a wheelbarrow across Niagara Falls; you have to believe enough to get in the wheelbarrow.

> *That if thou shalt confess with thy mouth the Lord Jesus, and shalt believe in thine heart that God hath raised him from the dead, thou shalt be saved. For with the heart man believeth unto righteousness; and with the mouth confession is made unto salvation. (Romans 10:9-10)*

Below is a sample prayer of repentance and faith which can serve as a guide to you if you wish to receive your salvation now.

A final word of encouragement is found in Psalm 116:12-13.

> *What shall I render unto the LORD for all his benefits toward me? I will take the cup of salvation, and call upon the name of the LORD.*

> *"Heavenly Father, have mercy on me, a sinner. I believe in you and that your Word is true. I believe that Jesus Christ is the Son of the living God and that He died on the cross so that I may now have forgiveness for my sins and eternal life.*
>
> *I believe in my heart that you, Lord God, raised Him from the dead. Please, Jesus, forgive me, for every sin I have ever committed or done in my heart, please, Lord Jesus, forgive me, and come into my heart as my personal Lord and Savior today.*
>
> *I give you my life and ask you to take full control from this moment on; I pray this in the name of Jesus Christ."*
>
> *Amen.*

PUBLIC CONFESSION

We cannot fail to note the statement from Romans that *"with the heart* man believeth unto righteousness; and *with the mouth* confession is made unto salvation" (Romans 10:10). Salvation is first a matter of the heart, but there is something about confessing your faith in Jesus out loud *with the mouth*, especially before other people, that changes an inner state into an outer reality. Water baptism is one obvious (and commanded) biblical way of doing this, but every opportunity to confess Jesus before men should be taken if you are to grow in your faith. Indeed, the words of Jesus in this regard are especially compelling.

> *Whosoever therefore shall confess me before men, him will I confess also before my Father which is in heaven. But whosoever shall deny me before men, him will I also deny before my Father which is in heaven. (Matthew 10:32-33)*

Assurance of Salvation

Even after receiving salvation you will struggle with sin. Overcoming the power of the evil one in our lives is a lifelong issue of growing in God's grace and is never complete until the resurrection. A key part of this struggle is holding on to your faith that you have indeed been saved even when you stumble and even when you don't feel like it. Prayer, Bible study, and especially Christian fellowship are important to your success. The most common thing in the world for a new Christian (and many old ones) is to not go to church because they don't feel worthy. Here is the solution to that problem: go anyway.

Always remember the words of the apostle John:

> *He that hath the Son hath life; and he that hath not the Son of God hath not life. These things have I written unto you that believe on the name of the Son of God; that ye may know that ye have eternal life, and that ye may believe on the name of the Son of God. (1 John 5:12-13)*

APPENDIX B:
THE BAPTISM WITH THE HOLY SPIRIT

In addition to the experience of being "born again," which is associated with conversion or salvation and water baptism, the Bible refers to a baptism with (or in) the Holy Spirit, a filling with the Holy Spirit, or the gift of the Holy Spirit. Over the centuries, different denominations have developed their own way of understanding these matters. Some baptize infants, claiming they are converted or saved by the faith of their parents. Such children later receive teaching of a catechism and are "confirmed." This practice is intended to give the individual a chance to make their own decision, although in practice many may just go through the motions to please family. Some denominations also consider this confirmation process to be the time the individual is baptized in the Holy Spirit.

Other denominations insist on adult individuals making their own decision about accepting Jesus as their personal Lord and Savior, typically by responding to an invitation at a public meeting and undergoing baptism as an adult. Many of these consider the Baptism with the Holy Spirit to be an automatic part of, and inseparable from, conversion. Others view the Baptism with the Holy Spirit as a separate, subsequent event. Most of these treat "speaking in tongues" as the primary sign associated with Baptism with the Holy Spirit.

In modern times, the first denominations to clearly teach the Baptism with the Holy Spirit and speaking in tongues were the Pentecostals in the early 1900s. In the 1970s, large numbers of individuals in other denominations moved in to similar understanding and experience. These people were and are called Charismatics. This Charismatic outpouring caused a great deal of controversy and division within existing denominations and churches and was even denounced as a counterfeit Christian experience by some.

Because many of those moving into the Pentecostal and Charismatic movements were broken into small groups led by isolated pastors of limited training, and because they tended to emphasize experience over doctrinal rigor, these groups gained a reputation for strange and idiosyncratic doctrines and practices and even cultish behavior. This is especially true in third world countries where the phenomenon has exploded. More recently, conflict between the older evangelical and newer charismatic groups has declined, with charismatic practices such as raising of hands and even dancing during worship being adopted by some evangelicals. Moreover, these groups often find themselves standing together in today's social and cultural battles. The term *evangecostals* has entered the lexicon.

It seems clear from scripture that while conversion itself is a work of the Holy Spirit, the church is also intended to be empowered by the indwelling Holy Spirit and for its evangelical work on earth. All Christians committed to this work should desire whatever gifts and empowering the Lord intends them to have. A prayerful seeking of such gifts is required. The following is a review of the relevant scripture references.

REVIEW OF SCRIPTURES

Matthew 3:11

> *I baptize you with water for repentance. But after me will come one who is more powerful than I, whose sandals I am not fit to carry. He will baptize you with the Holy Spirit and with fire.*

Jesus is the one who baptizes with the Holy Spirit.

John 16:5-16

This is a discussion of the work and purpose of the Holy Spirit in the church. The Holy Spirit could not come until Jesus left, and he says his followers are better off with the Spirit with them than with Jesus himself physically present. The Spirit convicts the world of sin and judgment in partnership with human evangelism. He will guide the disciples into all truth, even more than they could have borne at that time. This speaks of progressive revelation throughout the church age, as opposed to the idea that the early church had a complete revelation at the ascension. The Holy Spirit does not speak about himself, but testifies of Jesus on behalf of the Father.

Acts 1:8

> But you will receive power when the Holy Spirit comes on you; and you will be my witnesses in Jerusalem, and in Judea and Samaria, and to the ends of the earth.

The purpose is power associated with witnessing. The phrase, "ends of the earth," supports the expectation that this is for the present day as well as the first century, since the witnessing mission continues.

Acts 2

Speaking in tongues was the initial sign of the Baptism with the Holy Spirit. The tongues were actual languages understood by visitors. They declared the wonders of God. Their behavior made some think they were drunk. Peter declares this to be a sign spoken of by Joel. He follows with an evangelistic sermon resulting in three thousand saved and water baptized.

Acts 4:31

> After they prayed, the place where they were meeting was shaken. And they were all filled with the Holy Spirit and spoke the word with boldness.

After the initial Baptism with the Holy Spirit, the same believers could experience additional fillings with the Holy Spirit. Powerful testimony is again associated.

Acts 8:4-25

After Philip preached the gospel in Samaria, with signs of healing and casting out demons, with even the sorcerer Simon being converted, and after the converts were water baptized, they still had to send for Peter and John to lay hands on them to receive the Holy Spirit. The reason Peter and John were needed for this is not clear but may have been related to the initial opening on the gospel to the Samaritans. This also shows receiving the Baptism with the Holy Spirit to be an event distinct from salvation or conversion. Simon "saw" that the Holy Spirit was given by the laying on of the apostles' hands and coveted this power. Though just what he saw is not stated, it was presumably different than the healing and deliverance he had already seen, possibly (but not certainly) speaking in tongues.

Acts 10–11, Especially 10:44-47

While Peter was still speaking these words, the Holy Spirit came on all who heard the message. The circumcised believers who had come with Peter were astonished that the gift of the Holy Spirit had been poured out even on the Gentiles. For they heard them speaking in tongues and praising God. Then Peter said, Can anyone keep these people from being baptized with water? They have received the Holy Spirit just as we have.

God leads Peter to preach to the house of the Roman Cornelius. God spontaneously baptizes them in the Holy Spirit, with a manifestation of speaking in tongues and praising God. Apparently this was because Peter and the Jewish believers needed more convincing that salvation was for the Gentiles as well. Also, in this case, the Baptism with the Holy Spirit precedes water baptism and is near simultaneous with salvation/conversion.

Acts 11:15-17

As I began to speak, the Holy Spirit came on them as he had come on us at the beginning. Then I remembered what the Lord had said: John baptized with water, but you will be baptized with the Holy Spirit. So if God gave them the same gift as he gave us, who was I to think that I could oppose God? When they heard this, they had no further objections and praised God saying, So then, God has granted even the Gentiles repentance unto life.

Peter and the apostles took speaking in tongues and praising God as proof of the Baptism with the Holy Spirit, as well as of salvation.

Acts 19:6

When Paul placed his hands on them, the Holy Spirit came on them, and they spoke in tongues and prophesied.

Here Paul finds Gentile disciples of John the Baptist. He asks them if they had received the Spirit when they believed. He further instructed them about Jesus, they believed and were water baptized in Jesus' name. He laid hands on them, and they received the Holy Spirit with the manifestation of tongues and prophesying.

Thus, of the four recorded incidents of the Baptism with the Holy Spirit in Acts (Pentecost, Samaria, Cornelius, and Ephesus), tongues were a sign in three and possibly the fourth. The Baptism with the Holy Spirit occurs both before and after water baptism, always with or after salvation/conversion, and with and without the laying on of hands.

1 Corinthians 12:28-29

> *Now you are the body of Christ, and each one of you is a part of it. And in the church God has appointed first of all apostles, second prophets, third teachers, then workers of miracles, also those having gifts of healing, those able to help others, those with gifts of administration, and those speaking in different kinds of tongues. Are all apostles? Are all prophets? Are all teachers? Do all work miracles? Do all have gifts of healing? Do all speak in tongues? Do all interpret? But eagerly desire the greater gifts.*

Just as not all are apostles, not all speak in tongues. Thus one cannot be totally dogmatic about tongues and the Baptism with the Holy Spirit. However, this passage may refer to speaking in tongues with interpretation in the assembly, not in personal prayer. It concludes with an admonition to eagerly seek the greater gifts.

1 Corinthians 13:8-10

> *Love never fails. But where there are prophecies, they will cease; where there are tongues, they will be stilled…but when perfection comes, the imperfect disappears.*

This passage is used by some to argue that, with the completion of the New Testament canon, tongues and other first century signs ceased. However, the passage itself says that when that which is perfect (complete) comes, not only tongues but knowledge will pass away. Also, "I shall know fully, even as I am fully known" (1 Corinthians 13:12). This seems to better fit the Second Coming and end of the church age than the end of the first century.

1 Corinthians 14

This chapter contains a lengthy discussion on tongues, interpretation, and prophesying. The following are a few key points:

- Paul wants everyone to speak in tongues (1 Corinthians 14:5).
- Paul speaks in tongues more than all of them (1 Corinthians 14:18. See also Acts 9:17).
- He who speaks in tongues edifies himself (1 Corinthians 14:4).
- But he who prophesies (or interprets the tongues) edifies others (1 Corinthians 14:4-5).
- Tongue talkers and prophets have complete control of themselves (1 Corinthians 14:26-33).
- Do not forbid speaking in tongues (1 Corinthians 14:39).

Luke 11:11-13

> *Which of you fathers, if your son asks for a fish, will give him a snake instead? Or if he asks for an egg, will give him a scorpion? If you then, though you are evil, know how to give good gifts to your children, how much more will your Father in heaven give the Holy Spirit to those who ask him?*

We need not fear that we will get some demon if we ask to be baptized in the Holy Spirit.

CONCLUSION

The Baptism with the Holy Spirit, like water baptism, is a second event following salvation or conversion. It is a baptism or submergence in the Holy Spirit performed by Jesus on the believer by faith. Its purpose is not salvation but empowerment for the work of being his witnesses. Scriptural accounts of people being baptized in the Holy Spirit lead us to expect speaking in tongues and praising God to be the common initial manifestation. Christians wishing to be fully used of God in this age should earnestly seek the empowering scripture indicates is necessary.

APPENDIX C:
THE CHURCH

When Jesus came into the coasts of Caesarea Philippi, he asked his disciples, saying, Whom do men say that I the Son of man am? And they said, Some say that thou art John the Baptist: some, Elias; and others, Jeremias, or one of the prophets. He saith unto them, But whom say ye that I am?

And Simon Peter answered and said, Thou art the Christ, the Son of the living God. *And Jesus answered and said unto him, Blessed art thou, Simon Barjona: for flesh and blood hath not revealed it unto thee, but my Father which is in heaven. And I say also unto thee, That thou art Peter, and* upon this rock I will build my church; *and the gates of hell shall not prevail against it.*
—Matthew 16:13-18

An individual might be saved by calling upon the name of the Lord Jesus without a full theological understanding of who Jesus is, but the measure of the church is precisely how well it confesses who Jesus is.

And I fell at his feet to worship him. And he said unto me, See thou do it not: I am thy fellow servant, and of thy brethren that have the testimony of Jesus: worship God: for the testimony of Jesus is the spirit of prophecy. *(Revelation 19:10)*

The prophetic mission of the church on earth is to bear faithful witness concerning who Jesus is. A particular church establishment can have many failings, but if it fails in this regard it is ripe for judgment and even extinction.

In the New Testament we see this struggle over who Jesus is beginning to emerge as the following verses attest:

Hereby know ye the Spirit of God: Every spirit that confesseth that Jesus Christ is come in the flesh is of God: And every spirit that confesseth not that Jesus Christ is come in the flesh is not of God: and this is that spirit of antichrist, whereof ye have heard that it should come; and even now already is it in the world. (1 John 4:2-3)

For many deceivers are entered into the world, who confess not that Jesus Christ is come in the flesh. This is a deceiver and an antichrist. (2 John 1:7)

Beloved, when I gave all diligence to write unto you of the common salvation, it was needful for me to write unto you, and exhort [you] that ye should earnestly contend for the faith which was once delivered unto the saints. For there are certain men crept in unawares, who were before of old ordained to this condemnation, ungodly men, turning the grace of our God into lasciviousness, and denying the only Lord God, and our Lord Jesus Christ. (Jude 1:3-4)

Here we see the apostles John and Jude contesting with those who argued that Jesus was a spirit and did not come and die in the flesh. Similar disputes continued in the early centuries of the church. At the Council of Nicaea in 325 AD, from which we get the Nicaean Creed, the issue was whether the Son was just as much God as the Father was. At the Council of Ephesus in 431, the teachings of the Nestorians which held Christ to be close to God but not in union with him, and thus not "very god of very God," was condemned. This teaching dominated the Assyrian Church, sometimes called the Church of the East, and led to its separation from West and South. At the Council of Chalcedon in 451 the Monophysite doctrine that held Jesus to be a mixture of the divine and human natures but not really either one was similarly rejected. This Doctrine was also known as Monophysite or Jacobite and held sway in Egypt and Syria. The churches involved are called Oriental Orthodox or the Church of the South. Still later, the Western Roman Church and Eastern Orthodox Church split over the "Filioque," that says the Holy Spirit proceeds from both the Father and the Son, with the Eastern church holding to the Father only formulation. Again the dispute related to the nature of Jesus with the Eastern approach slightly demoting him with respect to the Father, or at least appearing to.

In each of these cases the issue was the nature of Christ, or, "Who do you say that I am?" In each case the churches which held the defective Christology were subsequently greatly diminished in power by the Moslems' conquest and in some cases completely wiped out. To date, in spite of all the other doctrinal issues dividing the Western church (Catholic, Protestant, etc.), it still holds to a correct Christology known as the Hypostatic Union. Jesus was and is 100 percent God and 100 percent man, the two natures in perfect union (with no daylight between them), yet without confusion (no mixture of the two natures into some kind of half God, half man). As a result, the Western church retains vitality and still assaults the gates of hell.

Yet this vitality is threatened by the issue of the extent of his lordship in the here and now. The Western church is at best ambivalent about asserting the absolute and total lordship of Jesus over the earth. She allows that man and his incarnation, the State, is in some sense a co-equal lord of a parallel sphere. She only confesses a partial lordship of Jesus Christ and is thus not bearing a true witness. Will she come under judgment for this the way her sister churches did? The danger is very real and early signs of judgment are all around. It is vital for the church to wake up to this error, repent, and again bear a full and faithful witness of her Lord.

So Which Church Is the Right One?

Few things bother people so much as all of the denominational differences in the church. How can we know who is right with so many divisions over so many issues? Is this the way it is supposed to be? Why can't we unite into one church? Is Christ divided? Here are two passages of scripture to consider when thinking about this issue:

For there must be also heresies among you, that they which are approved may be made manifest among you. (1 Corinthians 11:19)

Nevertheless the foundation of God standeth sure, having this seal, The Lord knoweth them that are his. And, Let everyone that nameth the name of Christ depart from iniquity. (2 Timothy 2:19)

Heresies and divisions are part of God's plan for separating the sheep from the goats. Some or all of this apparent confusion is necessary. The foundation of the church is nonetheless secure based on two things:

1. God knows who is his and who is just faking it. He is not fooled. The true church is the set of all born-again believers as seen by God in heaven, and this true church includes and excludes some people from all denominations and even outside of any visible organized church.

2. The thing for the individual to do is not to try and fix the disunity or figure out which church is the right one, but to "depart from iniquity." In other words, see that your own faith and morals line up with the Word.

The true church then is the set of people known to the Lord in heaven as his own. The visible church is not one denomination or the other but those who bear true witness to Jesus Christ and live their lives accordingly. It is on behalf of this church that Christ moves from heaven to bring about victory and vindication in history.

THE BRIDE OF CHRIST, WARTS AND ALL

In history, and in the present, visible church organizations are not all that pretty. But from Christ's point of view in heaven, the true church is a beautiful bride adorned and fit for her husband. It is for us to see the church the way Christ sees her, which is what she really is, and not as she appears to our darkened eyes in this world. If you love Christ, you must love his church, warts and all.

APPENDIX D:
CLASSICAL ESCHATOLOGIES

The book of Revelation and portions of the Gospels, Epistles, Daniel, and other prophets, contain passages that speak of the future and the end times. The study of these passages is known as eschatology. These passages have been subject to widely varying interpretations and endless controversy. A summary of some of the main schools of thought is provided below:

Preterism, from the Latin *praeter*, meaning "past," holds that the prophetic events were either all fulfilled with the fall of Jerusalem, or all except the Second Coming.

Idealism holds that the prophecies do not foretell specific historic events, but describe the general pattern of all events to take place in church history. It was originally suggested by the Catholic Church in the fifteenth century but has significant Protestant support today.

Historicism, which seems to have been popular in the early centuries, and which was the main position of the Protestant Reformers such as Luther, holds that the prophecies primarily relate to specific events in church history. The Reformers, for example, applied prophecies about the antichrist to the papacy. Since it treats most prophecies concerning Israel as applying to the church, historicism is also called replacement theology.

Futurism is a general category of interpretations that sees the prophecies as mostly concerned with future events, often thought to be imminent. It is basically the opposite of Preterism. Within futurism, the millennium referred to in Revelation 20 and the Great Tribulation of the Gospels are the subject of a number of schools of thought themselves.

Premillennialism holds that Christ's Second Coming ushers in a literal reign of Christ and the church on earth for one thousand years, followed by a final rebellion of sinners and a final judgment. Coupled with this view are three ideas about the Great Tribulation and the associated rapture[40] of the church. Pre, mid, and post tribulationalism have to do with when the church will be raptured with respect to a seven year period of intense persecution that will immediately precede Christ's Second Coming. This school of thought is associated with a theological view known as dispensationalism and has been dominant in evangelical circles since the late nineteenth century. It is also associated with a literalist hermeneutic and with Christian Zionism which supports the Jewish State of Israel.

Amillennialism treats the millennium of Revelation 20 as entirely symbolic and unrelated to specific events. It is held by many main line Protestant denominations and tends to be pessimistic about the church's prospects prior to Christ's return.

Postmillennialism sees the millennium as symbolically showing the church being progressively more victorious, converting more people and discipling more nations over time. They either see the thousand years as symbolic of this whole church age or as the last and most successful thousand. Most hold to a final apostasy before the Second Coming, but some discount it, expecting Christ to come after a total church-led victory.

---

40. 1 Thessalonians 4:13-18. The rapture is the bodily taking up of Christians to meet Christ in the air at his coming.

Appendix E:
Economics

The idea that the economic behavior of people can be described in terms of economic laws aligns with Natural Law thinking. It implies that we have to view human economic behavior as governed by pre-existing laws which we discover through observation and reasoning, much as we do physical laws. This treats economic law as "God given" and not subject to idealistic alteration. This view is offensive to rebellious man who wishes to create a different economic order according to his own lights. We see this in the communist desire to create "new soviet man," with modified thinking that fits in with their ideal society. We often hear market theorists denounced as "ideologues" by politicians bent on imposing their own socialist ideology on a reluctant reality.

The history of rebellious man's efforts to impose his idealistic economic systems contrary to the way God made man and the world is long and unhappy. Poverty, starvation, and fighting over supposedly scarce resources have invariably been the result.

God created the world for man and endowed it with abundant resources. There is no real scarcity of land, energy, or material resources as a fundamental fact. Scarcity results from failure to follow God's law on the part of rebellious man. Scarcity is often engineered by would be man-gods as part of their power grab. The reality is one of providential abundance.

God created man, the world, and the true economic order. Large portions of scripture are dedicated to elucidating God's laws and principles on economic matters. Economics are therefore an important area for Christians to understand if they are to cause the laws of their nations to conform to God's law. Economics is too important to be left to the economists.

Definition: *An economy is a whole bunch of people running around, producing and exchanging goods and services.*

When people are efficiently and effectively producing and exchanging large volumes of goods and services, the economy is strong, and wealth and opportunity are abundant. The role of godly government is to create and maintain an environment conducive to this.

All economic activity starts when entrepreneurs and investors decide that particular economic activities are likely to be profitable. They must first have some wealth accumulated from savings. They must put this wealth, which they could otherwise enjoy immediately, at risk in some business enterprise. They will do so if they judge that the future wealth to be enjoyed will be large enough to justify the wait and the risk. They thus always make a risk/reward calculation. If government reduces risk by such things as enforcing contracts, protecting private property rights, and suppressing crime, and increases rewards by such things as tax rate reduction, more potential business activity will make sense and more will occur.

Being an entrepreneur is very difficult. Being a successful one is even more so. Relatively few people have what it takes to succeed. The economic wellbeing of a society is highly dependent on these few individuals. It is therefore to everyone's advantage to encourage them. When entrepreneurs and investors are actively starting and expanding businesses, jobs are plentiful, and workers can command good wages. When workers become envious of wealthy investors and ask government to transfer some of the investors' wealth to them, they cut their own throats.

It is useful to make a distinction between risk and uncertainty. Uncertainty refers to the likelihood of the government changing the rules. If rules, laws, tax rates, and such are subject to change, the risk/reward calculation becomes difficult or impossible. Investors and entrepreneurs will defer starting or expanding businesses until the uncertainty is removed. This is why businessmen like political gridlock. Governments that create a stable environment of laws, regulations, and tax rates encourage economic activity. Governments that float radical proposals for change cause business to wait for stability, slowing economic activity.

Money is any commodity widely accepted and easily moved around. Gold and silver are natural money because they are commodities having stable value, are sufficiently rare that small quantities can be used to buy most things, are easily assayed, and are formed into the convenient shape of coins which resist corrosion. By using gold and silver coins, the exchange of goods and services becomes much easier than bartering so many chickens for a pair of shoes. Easy exchange allows specialization, which increases productivity.

Paper money and bank accounts are even more convenient than moving physical gold and silver around. However, they are more subject to counterfeiting and manipulation by governments. A cartoon shows counterfeiters in a boiler room saying, "The local economy is about to get a much needed shot in the arm." Government-led inflation of the money supply works much like counterfeiting; the new money gets its value by diluting value out of the money in your pocket. The first to receive the new money benefit the most from it. Eventually it works its way through the economy, the stimulation of the economy wears off, wages and prices all rise, and there is no real gain in the production and exchange of goods and services. Attempting to stimulate the economy by inflation is akin to attempting to make a sick person well by giving the person stimulants. What should be done for a sick person is to get them healthy with things like proper rest, good diet, and proper exercise. This is analogous to implementing healthy economic policies of sound money, predictable law and regulation, and low taxes.

Economists tend to make things seem more complicated than they are. Part of this stems from the desire to "be as God," manipulating the lives of other men, playing the role of "benefactor" in their own minds. Far better policies result from conforming economic policies and laws to the principles in God's law. These include,

1. Protecting innocent life and property.

2. Providing for honest money.

3. Upholding contracts without favoritism.

For many Christians, compassion for the poor is a major consideration. Some consider it the primary yard stick for judging economic policy. It makes superficial sense to see the wide disparity between the rich and the poor, and some see taking money from the rich and giving it to the poor as an obvious solution. The problem with this thinking is that the rich usually get that way through sustained "good economic behavior" such as hard work, education, saving, and prudent management of resources. The poor often get poor through the opposite "bad economic behavior." Thus, in practice, taking from the rich to give to the poor largely amounts to punishing good economic behavior and rewarding bad economic behavior. This is not the road to a better economic future. In Romans 13 and 1 Peter 2:14, we are told that government is given to punish wrong doing and reward well doing. It is wise to focus our laws on encouraging the behavior we want rather than forcing a result we want. If we are unhappy with the results, such as income disparity, we should look to improving opportunity for "well doers" rather than seeking to change the results after the fact.

APPENDIX F:
THE WITCHCRAFT OF WORDS

O foolish Galatians, who hath bewitched you, that ye should not obey the truth,
before whose eyes Jesus Christ hath been evidently set forth, crucified among you?
—Galatians 3:1

Philosophy is a battle against the bewitchment *of our intelligence by means of language.*
—Philosopher Ludwig Wittgenstein

We *communicate* in words, but we also *think* in words. Words can be used to illuminate an issue in the service of truth or to obfuscate an issue in the service of lies. Liars are really good at this. A good liar can talk you out of the money in your pocket, the shirt off your back, and the blood out of your veins. And they don't even have to lie, exactly. They just have be clever about how they say things, what they include, what they leave out, what words they use to evoke the right sub-rational emotional response, how they push your buttons.

Today, Americans have lost most of their rights to their money, their property, their privacy, their children and families, their opinions, and their religion. These rights have not been taken by force; rather, Americans have been talked into giving them up freely. Who would have believed it?

HOW IT'S DONE

There are many techniques in the witchcraft of words. Here are a few:

Made-up and loaded words. *Underprivileged:* A privilege is something you have over and above what you are due, so can you have less privilege than you deserve? *Access to:* Access to health care or access to abortion, when what is meant is not that someone is denied access but that they want someone else to pay for it. *Homophobic* (or anything-phobic): Here the psychiatric term for a mental illness called a phobia is appended to something to make opposition to it sound like a mental illness and thus cut off debate.

Name calling, ridicule, and slander. *Racist, sexist, anti-gay, one percenter, anti-science, religious fanatic, misogynist*. No one likes being called names, and no one wants to associate with the victim of name-calling lest they be called names too. This seems ridiculously childish, but it works.

The big lie. *Right wingers killed Kennedy, Matthew Shepherd was killed because he was gay, women only make 76 percent of what men do for the same work, and the constitutional wall of separation between church and state*. This technique was famously used by the Nazis who found that people will often believe a big lie repeated often enough because their normal skepticism is on the lookout for little sneaky lies. A big lie brazenly repeated takes them off guard. "No one would say something that outrageous if it wasn't true," they think.

Appeal to authority. *Studies prove, experts agree, 95 percent of scientists believe, three out of four doctors recommend, Einstein said, it is universally agreed*. You see this a lot when the subject is something like evolution or global warming where a mastery of the facts is difficult for the average person to obtain.

PC language. *Calling policemen "police-persons," calling promiscuity "being sexually active," calling child killing "women's health care," saying "significant other" instead of husband or wife*. By forcing everyone to change the words they use to describe things they force everyone to think differently about them without realizing it or thinking about it.

Glittering generalities. *Who can be against diversity, inclusion, affirming people, or leadership?* When the case for sin is made in terms of glittering generalities instead of specifics, you don't know how to respond.

Incantation. *These slogans, glittering generalities, and loaded words are repeated endlessly*. No room is allowed for discussion and debate. The effect is mind numbing, almost like casting a spell.

GEORGE ORWELL'S *1984*

Here is an excerpt from George Orwell's famous book *1984* in which he describes how a totalitarian state uses the witchcraft of words, which Orwell called "Newspeak," to control the minds of the population:

Don't you see that the whole aim of Newspeak is to narrow the range of thought? In the end we shall make thought-crime literally impossible, because there will be no words in which to express it. Every concept that can ever be needed will be expressed by exactly one word, with its meaning rigidly defined and all its subsidiary meanings rubbed out and forgotten. . . . Has it ever occurred to you, Winston, that by the year 2050, at the very latest, not a single human being will be alive who could understand such a conversation as we are having now?[41]

THE SIMPLE

Psalms and Proverbs have many warnings about *the simple*. These are people who lack wisdom and are the natural prey of liars. We are all *the simple* until we gain wisdom, and we gain wisdom from the fear of God and the Word of God. We are admonished to gain wisdom above all things; its worth is more than silver or hidden treasure. Those who reject the wisdom of God in his Word remain simple, no matter how many degrees or accomplishments they have. They remain easy prey for the practitioners of the witchcraft of words. Don't be simple.

BEHIND THE WORDS

As powerful as the witchcraft of words may be, it does not account for the full extent of madness we see around us today. People believe without question that a child in the womb one minute before birth is not human in any sense. They believe that a man who says he is a woman is a woman. They believe that because the movies show 110 pound women routinely beating up 250 pound men that this, rather than their own contrary experience, is reality. They believe that government debt can grow forever without consequences, that violent criminals and terrorists are the good guys, and that the police and American soldiers are the bad guys. There has to be more to this than just charlatans being clever with words.

From the time of Nimrod, the Pharaohs, Nebuchadnezzar, and Nero, to the time of the French Revolution, the Nazis, and the Communists, and up to our present crisis, the political totalitarians have

---

41. George Orwell, *1984* (London: Penguin Books, 1949).

always been associated with the occult. Practices such as child sacrifice and deviant sexual practices are not just personal moral failures but stock in trade for the occult. Occultists believe they can tap into greater power by conducting such transgressive practices, and power is the lure and objective of witchcraft and the occult practices. Behind the witchcraft of words lies something more fundamental and darker, and that is *actual witchcraft*.

Paul tells us in Ephesians 6:12 that our Christian warfare is not principally against flesh and blood but against "powers and principalities ... in high places." When Daniel fasted and prayed for revelation he was given a glimpse of the celestial struggle between Michael, the Prince of Persia, and the Prince of Greece, angelic beings associated with the earthly political entities of Israel, Persia, and Greece. We are told that in the end the church will sit in judgment of fallen angels.

All of this tells us that there is a battle of some kind taking place between angelic beings behind the scene of our visible human political struggles. Paul again tells us in 2 Corinthians 10:4 that the weapons we have for this warfare are powerful, casting down imaginations and every high thing that exalts itself against the knowledge of God. So our battle is against fallen angels and the battleground is the minds of men.

You may be sure that on the other side there are people in the occult in active association with these fallen angels, seeking to keep people lost in confusion. Only the church by means of Spirit-led prayer and warfare worship can oppose this spiritual and occult activity. In that battle we should see our human adversaries primarily as captives of our true satanic adversary and seek their liberation into the light of the gospel when possible.

> *And the servant of the Lord must not strive; but be gentle unto all men, apt to teach, patient, In meekness instructing those that oppose themselves; if God peradventure will give them repentance to the acknowledging of the truth; And that they may recover themselves out of the snare of the devil, who are taken captive by him at his will.*
> *(2 Timothy 2:24-26)*

You do not, however, see Paul or the other apostles running around rebuking and cursing these fallen angels or even engaging them directly, as is the manner in some churches today. Indeed, Jude verses 9 and 10 would seem to advise against this practice. Rather, as the battle is in the mind, we war against these spirits by prayer, preaching, and sound study and exposition of the Word of God.

To these practices I would add that pastors should note examples of the witchcraft of words in the media and point them out to their congregations, teaching them how to identify these manipulative arts and avoid being enchanted.

APPENDIX G:
RESOURCES

The following websites are useful for further research.

Theology, Philosophy, and Reformation
www.chalcedon.edu/blog/blog.php
www.americanvision.org/

History
www.christianhistorystore.com/

Science, Creation, and Evolution
http://crev.info/

Abortion and Life Issues
www.abortionno.org/ (Caution: Graphic)

Homosexuality
http://narth.com/
http://pfox.org/

Christian Persecution Worldwide
http://www.persecution.com/

Christian Persecution in America
http://www.aclj.org/

Christian Education
http://www.achipa.com/
http://www.hslda.org/
http://www.homeschool.com/

Revival
http://www.thecall.com/

News
http://www.wnd.com/
http://www.lucianne.com/
http://www.realclearpolitics.com/

INDEX

A

Abel, 34, 39

Abraham, 36

Alexander, 28, 45, 52

Alexis de Tocqueville, 59

anarchy, 40, 51, 53, 97

antediluvian, 35

Aquinas, 45, 46, 47

Aristotle, 45, 46, 47, 89

astrologers, 38

atheists, 13, 1, 21, 79

Augustine, 43, 44, 45, 46

B

Babel, 36, 79

Babylon, 26, 27, 38

C

Caesar, 11, 25, 29, 64, 97

capital punishment, 35, 71, 72, 83, 86

Chalcedon, 42, 114, 129

Christopher Columbus, 50

civil government, 35, 50, 51, 59, 64, 65, 66, 67, 68, 74, 86

civil justice, 77

Congregationalism, 50

Connecticut, 51

Constantine, 42

constitution, 51, 55, 66, 69, 70

Constitution (US), 51, 54, 55, 57, 59, 66, 69, 70

constitutional federal republic, 69

Constitutional Federal Republic, 49, 50

Counter Reformation, 48

Cyrus, 28, 38

D

Daniel, 3, 27, 28, 38, 117, 126

Darius, 28

David, 3, 4, 21, 37, 38, 53, 90, 94

Deconstructionism, 57

deistic, 26

democracy, 11, 28, 29, 68, 69, 70

devil, 10, 32, 34, 83, 86, 87, 103, 126

dietary laws, 35

dominion, 31, 33, 34, 35, 60, 63, 65

dualism, 44, 100

E

education, 12, 57, 61, 76, 86, 90, 91, 122, 129

empire, 27, 28, 29, 38, 39, 41, 42, 61, 79, 80

Empire, 2, 11, 28, 29, 30, 38, 41, 42, 43, 48, 60, 61, 62, 79, 80, 94, 101

Enlightenment, 47, 52, 56, 93

Episcopalianism, 50

epistemology, 22, 23, 45, 47, 56, 57

evolution, 1, 2, 22, 30, 124

F

family, 35, 36, 61, 65, 66, 71, 75, 83, 89, 100, 107

Filioque, 43, 114

French Revolution, 47, 52, 53, 93, 125

Fundamental Orders of Connecticut, 51

G

gardener, 31

Gödel, 56

Great Awakening, 52

Great Schism, 43

Greek, 2, 28, 29, 38, 45, 46, 60

guilt, 34, 49, 103

H

Hellenic, 28, 38

Holy Spirit, 7, 10, 12, 31, 32, 40, 41, 43, 61, 85, 95, 97, 99, 107, 108, 109, 110, 111, 112, 114

Huguenots, 52

humanistic philosophy, 10, 26, 46, 47, 56

Hypostatic Union, 115

I

interest, 75

International Law, 81

interposition, 53

Israel, 3, 4, 36, 39, 40, 67, 81, 94, 117, 118, 126

J

Jacobite, 42, 114

Jamestown, 50

Jesus, 5, 6, 9, 10, 11, 12, 13, 19, 20, 21, 29, 30, 38, 39, 40, 42, 49, 53, 59, 60, 61, 64, 65, 67, 75, 79, 80, 85, 89, 94, 95, 96,

98, 100, 101, 103, 104, 105, 106, 107, 108, 111, 112, 113, 114, 115, 116, 123

L

Law of Nations, 80, 81, 82
Legal Positivism, 80, 81
legislature, 36, 58, 70, 71
limitation of liability, 77
Luther, 48, 86, 87, 117

M

Mary, 21, 29
Mayflower Compact, 51
Medo-Persian Empire, 28
middle ages, 43, 44, 45, 95
Modernism, 56, 57, 58
monopoly, 77

N

Natural Law, 80, 81, 119
Nebuchadnezzar, 26, 28, 125
Nestorians, 114
Nicene Creed, 43
Noah, 34, 35

O

Orthodox, 42, 114

P

Parliament, 50, 53, 55
parliamentary, 55, 70
persecution, 11, 12, 41, 42, 51, 61, 86, 89, 90, 94, 95, 99, 100, 118, 129
Pharaoh, 36, 97
Pilgrims, 50, 51
Platonic, 44
post-modern, 26
Postmodernism, 57
predestination, 27
Presbyterianism, 50
Puritans, 50, 51

R

Reformation, 47, 48, 50, 52, 53, 93, 129
Renaissance, 43, 45, 46, 47, 48, 52, 56, 93
republic, 11, 62, 70
Republic, 29, 59, 71
restitution, 40, 71, 73
resurrection, 39, 49, 61, 62, 106
Rome, 28, 41, 42, 43, 48

S

salvation, 16, 17, 19, 20, 23, 27, 29, 39, 54, 61, 65, 97, 103, 104, 105, 106, 107, 109, 110, 111, 112, 114

Samuel, 37, 53

Satan, 32, 34

Saul, 37, 53

Solomon, 37

sovereignty, 37, 54, 55, 64, 69

T

theosis, 43

tyranny, 40, 68, 79, 97

U

United Nations, 79, 81

W

woman, 33, 34, 38, 61, 88, 89, 125

worship, 1, 30, 32, 34, 50, 61, 65, 70, 82, 96, 102, 108, 113, 126

Z

zodiac, 35

www.ingramcontent.com/pod-product-compliance
Lightning Source LLC
Chambersburg PA
CBHW072126090426
42739CB00012B/3080